MEDWORDS
(Conversations with Animal Guides)

by

Verna Safran

Copyright © 1999, 2001 by Verna Safran

All rights reserved.
No part of this book may be reproduced, restored in a retrieval system, or transmitted by means, electronic, mechanical, photocopying, recording, or otherwise, without written consent from the author.

ISBN: 1-58721-965-4

Cover design by Lynne Knight

1stBooks - rev. 1/29/01

MEDWORDS
(Conversations with Animal Guides)

TABLE OF CONTENTS

Chapter	Chapter Title	Page
	INTRODUCTION	ix
1	(A Parent's Death) THE RAVEN	1
2	(Prosperity) THE BLUEJAY	7
3	(Writer's Block) THE BEAVER	11
4	(Fame and Success) THE BEE	15
5	(Handling Stress) THE CAMEL	21
6	(A Head for Business) OWL AND RHINOCEROS	25
7	(Leaving a Sinking Ship) THE RAT	31
8	(Adjusting to New Surroundings) THE RED ANT	39
9	(Making New Friends) THE GREY WOLF	47
10	(Acceptance versus Individuality) THE EAGLE	55
11	(Acquiring Wisdom) THE CORAL SNAKE	61
12	(Making Choices, Gaining Focus) THE GREAT BLUE HERON	67

13	(Being a Teacher) THE MALLARD	73
14	(Strength in Misfortune) THE BEAR	81
15	(Telling the Universe) THE PRAYING MANTIS	89
16	(Abundance) THE WHITE-TAILED DEER	95
17	(Dealing with Difficult People) THE ARMADILLO	103
18	(Love versus Control) THE SPIDER	109
19	(Unlucky in Love) THE FROG	115
20	(No Place Like Home) DR. RABBIT	121
21	(Finding a Life Partner) THE TURTLE DOVE	127
22	(Affirmations on Lovability) THE RED FOX	131
23	(Dumping a Bad Habit) THE SALAMANDER	137
24	(Healer in the Sky) THE PEREGRINE FALCON	141
25	(Contentment) THE MOUSE	145
26	(Activism) THE GADFLY	149
27	(Aging) THE ALLIGATOR	155
28	(Work as Play) THE OTTERS	161

29	(Responsibility) THE FLORIDA PANTHER	165
30	(Dealing with Mortality) THE BUTTERFLY	171
EPILOGUE		177

INTRODUCTION

It was an artist friend from Canada who first taught me how to meditate. When she was staying with me in New York, she got up in the morning, opened her Bible, then sat on the floor with her eyes closed and did deep breathing. I asked her what she was doing. "I'm getting my marching orders," she said. Since she was Catholic, she meditated on Scripture. She would choose a line from the Bible at random, then stay with it during a period of deep relaxation for at least fifteen or twenty minutes, until she felt she had been given God's command for the day.

She asked me if I'd like to try it. I preferred to just do the breathing, relaxation and concentration, and see what came to me. My first experience was indeed remarkable. It was a very clear dream-like vision, which I can still see to this day. There was a knight in armor, sitting under a tree, resting. He was part of the Crusades, and in the distance, I could see the spires of Jerusalem. Some of the other soldiers were nearby. The knight was a little worried, since he had lost contact with Charlemagne, who was leading the march. Wearily, the knight pushed back his helmet, to reveal – the knight was me! Then the other knights gathered around and said that since Charlemagne could not be found, that I should take his place. I put my helmet back on, and mounted my horse, rallying the others to proceed to the holy city.

This led me to ponder several questions: (1) What is my "Crusade"? What do I feel passionately about? (2) What is my "Jerusalem"? What is my ultimate goal? (3) Who is my "Charlemagne"? What leader(s) do I most admire? (4) Do I feel ready to be a leader myself? My mother once told me, when I was little, that she had conferred with my teacher, who told her that I had no leadership ability, and that if the true leader were absent, I could take over temporarily. This stayed with me my whole life (what little girl can argue with her mother and her teacher?) so I declined any office ever offered to me. This meditation seemed to be a turning point in my own self-understanding, a willingness to assume responsibility and take risks.

Some people prefer to just make their mind a blank and use the meditation process as a form of relaxation, my artist-mentor told me. But if you believe there is a helpful force or spirit in the universe, you can use it to get in touch with that force or spirit for guidance.

Fascinated with this process, I bought a book on meditation and learned some techniques for entering a new state of consciousness, or what the Buddhists call "no-mind." The suggestion I liked best was the one that said, "Go in your mind to a peaceful place, your favorite scene of natural beauty." For me, having grown up in New York State, that was the woods.

But then an interesting thing started happening. I would go, in meditation, to the woods, and ask the universe for help on a particular subject. At first, I received an image of a spirit guide in human form. Perhaps he was the long-lost soul-twin some mythologies say we all have. He looked to me like Apollo – youthful, radiant, resplendent, in gold and silver. Some might call him a guardian angel. I'm not sure I believe in angels, but I made a decision to accept as a gift whatever my meditations brought. The youth would speak a sentence or a word, and then disappear. But I wanted more than this remote, otherworldly figure. I wanted a conversation, a debate on problems close to my heart.

A year later, I visited my Canadian artist friend in Vancouver, and had the occasion to visit the Museum of Anthropology. Inside, were displays of Native American artifacts, drawings and sculptures. Outside, standing tall against the landscape, were huge totem poles. I sat beneath a Haida totem pole for an hour, perhaps longer – I'd lost all track of time. All I knew was that I was filled with a reverential awe at the experience: The larger-than-life height; the intensity, the scariness of those hollow eyes; the bold colors; the juxtaposition of man and animal forms; the reaching, reaching up into the unknown. I truly felt I was in the presence of Spirit.

I decided then to do what many Native Americans do when they meditate: Attempt to contact an animal spirit or totem for guidance and power.

And miraculously, after that, when I meditated, I too began encountering animals, birds, insects, who spoke to me on a topic of my choice. Were they merely figments of a creative writer's imagination? Or were they channelers, spiritual guides, sent to me to help me with a particular problem? In the spirit of gratitude and acceptance, I began writing down the conversations I had with my creature guides, calling them "Medwords" – short for "Meditation" and/or "Medicine" words. Since they said so many wise things, I've decided to share their insights, in the hope they may help other seekers like myself.

CHAPTER ONE
THE RAVEN
(A Parent's Death)

My mother was dying. She was 86 years old and she had decided to starve herself to death. I didn't know, at first, that this was her plan. All I knew was that this stout little woman, who had always been overweight, had slimmed down to a mere shadow of herself, and had lost interest in just about everything, including food.

Several years before, she went blind, from macular degeneration. She had been a legal secretary her whole life and her main interests were in reading and writing. She was an inveterate letter writer and wrote letters to the editor on every conceivable subject. She had also been the secretary of a discussion group. When she lost her eyesight, she made up her mind that she might as well die. And when my mother made up her mind about anything, she usually got her way.

It was when I noticed the wall calendar near her telephone that I caught on to her plan. There was nothing written on it for the month of February. There was just a black check mark, made with a magic marker, on the first of February, 1989. When I saw that she was ignoring the "Meals on Wheels" I had ordered delivered for her, saw that they were piling up in her refrigerator and that she had bought no food at all for several weeks, the significance of the black checkmark became apparent.

I had always had a difficult relationship with my mother. She was domineering, controlling, invasive. But as the older of two daughters, and the one that lived where my mother lived, in New York City, while my sister lived on the West Coast, I was the one appointed as caretaker. I resolved to do my duty.

But what was my duty here? I wondered. Jewish ethics prescribe that the highest value of them all is Life. Should I try to keep my mother alive as long as possible? Or should I accede to her wishes and allow her to die? My dilemma was made more difficult by the fact that everybody I spoke to seemed to have a different opinion. Her neighbors thought I should put her in a rest home. That would absolve them from any responsibility for her wellbeing. But she did not want to go to a rest home. She wanted to stay right where she was, in her own apartment, living with the memories of her departed husband. The neighbors, mostly elderly like my Mom, thought I was a bad daughter because I did not come and visit every day. They thought I was not taking care of her properly, and they told me so. But every time my mother and I were together, we argued. Various friends suggested I move in with her. That, for me, would have been self-destructive.

Her doctors – and she had many different doctors – one for each part of her body – did what they felt they were supposed to do, they prescribed medications. She had pills for her heart condition, drops for her eyes, tablets to help her sleep, pills for the pains she complained of in her stomach. My son worked out a system of marking the bottles with tape, so she would know which bottle was which. One thing I knew I could do, was make sure she took her medications. But I wondered if I should even do that. After awhile, my mother refused to go to the doctors any more. I sensed she was suffering from depression, but she would never admit that, so it was impossible to get her psychiatric help.

I tried getting a home health worker to shop and cook for her, and help her bathe, but my mother didn't want anyone there, and made things so impossible for each helper that she quit. We went through a string of aides – old women, young women, black women, white women. My mother still avoided eating by telling the helper she'd already eaten and was not hungry.

I tried to interest her in going to activities at the Senior Center, which was right in the same building where she lived. "I'm not interested in Activities," she said. Most of her friends had moved away or died, and she refused to talk to her only surviving sister.

I was becoming a nervous wreck. I was living in Brooklyn, and every time the "Lifeline" signal went off, I had to get in my car and drive into Manhattan to see what was going on with my mother, whether she'd fallen down or was too weak to move. I tried going to a therapist to help me resolve my feelings about what to do, but the therapist spent most of the time discussing whether I should sit up or lie down, and wanted me to tell him about my childhood instead of helping me deal with the here-and-now.

I knew I would not be able to cope with this complex situation unless I relaxed, and so I tried meditation. I went to my favorite peaceful place – a clearing in the woods. And there I met my first animal guide.

* * *

Actually, it is a bird. A raven, to be exact. Not a morose and gloomy one, such as the one who visited Edgar Allen Poe, but a rather sprightly and cheerful one.

"What are you so happy about, you black harbinger of death?" I yell at the bird.

"Death is nothing to get upset about," the raven says. "It's a perfectly natural occurrence."

"Death is loss," I tell the raven. "I guess you wouldn't understand that."

"I understand that some creatures must die," the raven says, "In order that some of us may live."

"Well, we don't eat carrion," I snap at him. "That's where you and I are different."

"Don't you?"

"Of course not!" I reply. "We are civilized creatures. We don't cannibalize each other!"

"Not even symbolically?" the raven persists.

"Well, of course there's that business of the blood and body of Christ at communion. But I don't believe in that."

"Is there no part of your mother that you wish to take and make part of yourself?"

This question startles me. Ravens are good at startling people.

"No!" I cry. "I hate the woman. She did her best to destroy my life – criticized me, ridiculed me, my whole life. It's because of her I was so insecure that my marriage failed and my friendships faltered. I'm only happy when I'm away from her!"

"I see," the raven says.

"What do you see?" I ask.

"I see that your hatred is preventing you from letting her go."

I breathe deeply and count to ten. "I'm doing my duty," I say. "I believe it is my duty to keep her alive."

The raven peers at me with his beady eyes. "Are you keeping her alive for your sake or for her sake?"

"I don't know what you mean," I sulk.

"She obviously wants to die," the raven says. "Why do you need to keep her with you?"

I came here to relax, and the raven is making me even more nervous than I was before. I decide, however, to receive him as a messenger of Higher Power, and resolve to take his questions seriously and answer them the best I can. "I'm afraid that people will accuse me of killing her," I reveal to the raven. "They're already regarding me as a murderer."

"No one said anything about killing her," the raven explains. "Just about letting her go. I suspect, however, that there have been times that you wanted to kill her."

Now I am really upset and start to shout. "How dare you!" I cry. "How dare you say such a thing!"

"True or not true?" the raven challenges.

"Of course, there are times when everyone gets angry –"

"And you are so afraid of your anger, that you are bending over backwards to hide it. Perhaps this anger is preventing you from dealing with what needs to be dealt with at this time."

"Which is?"

"Helping your mother to make the transition."

I get up and walk around a little. I pick up a dry twig and break it. The transition. It is a transition for the both of us, my mother and myself.

"How can I do that?" I ask.

"Resolving what needs to be resolved between you, perhaps," the raven says.

"There are maybe one or two things I do admire about her," I admit.

"Have you ever told her that?" queries the raven.

"No, why should I? She's never once complimented me."

"Perhaps now is the time," the raven says. We pause for a moment and glare at each other. I notice that the raven's blue-black feathers are glossy as silk and quite beautiful. "And what are these couple of things?" the raven prods me.

"She's good with words," I hesitantly begin.

"And so are you," suggests the raven. "Perhaps you will write what she never got the chance to."

"She's got a lot of friends. Friends who don't know how horrible she can – "

"We're thinking of positive things today," the raven reminds me. "Friends. You can be charming and helpful to people, and make your home a gathering place for friends."

"She's always been healthy. Never missed a day's work in her life. Works very hard."

"Admirable indeed," the raven says. "These qualities can live on in you."

Now that I've gotten started, I can think of many more of my mother's traits that – if I were not her daughter and her victim – I might want for myself. She's a good manager of money, practical and economical. Unless it's people within her own family, she is a champion of the underdog.

I realize that if I do take the raven's advice and make these qualities a part of me, it will be a way of giving my mother immortality. And so I may be better able to accept her departure.

"Are you feeling any better?" the raven asks me.

"The past few weeks have been hell," I respond. "I'm running out of energy."

"You must take care of yourself," the raven says. "No sense two people getting sick over this. And you are going to need your health in the next few weeks."

"But what shall I do?" I cry. "What is a good daughter to do?"

"Put her in God's hands," the raven advises.

* * *

I went on vacation for a week. I rested on the beach and bathed in the comforting water. My sense of calm restored, I returned to the city and found my mother confined to her bed. She did not even want to talk with anyone on the telephone. She had bedsores, and her body was almost skeletal in appearance. I put her in Mt. Sinai Hospital with "Do Not Resuscitate" orders and the request not to put her on feeding tubes. My mother thanked me. "You did the right thing," she said. I think it was the only compliment she ever gave me.

I went to visit her every day, bringing her ice cream, the only food she would eat. She was not a religious person, so there was no religious leader I could bring to her to discuss the end of life. I did bring a blind woman I knew, who came with her seeing-eye dog. My mother more or less made her last confession to her, telling her that she felt her blindness was a punishment for all the things she had done wrong, particularly as a mother. My mother and I had never said "I love you." It would have been a lie. But we did manage to make amends. Within two weeks, she passed away peacefully. It was March 9th. If I had left her in the hands of God a little earlier, she would have accomplished her secret mission on February 1.

I spent three months sorting through my parents' things before selling their apartment. It was a very healing process for me. My parents, having come through the Depression, were unable to give much, in either a tangible or intangible way. I found comfort and pleasure in giving away their things to people who could best make use of them. I wanted very little that was theirs, except, perhaps, the letters and photos. And the qualities of character they had passed along to me. I was now free to get about my work and lead my own life.

CHAPTER TWO
THE BLUEJAY
(Prosperity)

The cost of living in New York was beginning to make me crazy. I couldn't afford to eat out, or to go to the city's many cultural attractions which I once enjoyed. The only people I knew who hadn't left the city were highly successful in their professional fields and lived in rent-controlled apartments. So I went into the woods again, to sit beneath my meditation tree, this time to ask, "How can I get more money?"

* * *

A bluejay appears (Is it only possible to take advice on this subject from a thief?) and putting down a diamond (or rhinestone?) necklace in front of me, he responds:

"I've lived in these woods my whole life, and have never seen money growing on trees."

"Great," I mumble. "A wiseguy who trafficks in platitudes."

"I steal what I can use," the bluejay responds, "and advise you to do the same. Do you want to hear what I have to say or not?"

"I'm not sure. But I guess I do."

"Money is a scarce item. You have to scratch for it."

"Scratch?"

"Like truffles," says the bluejay, who has the disconcerting habit of not looking at me while he speaks.

"Are you suggesting I become a pig?" I ask.

"Money is not a pleasant subject," the bluejay says, "but you're the one who brought it up."

"Okay, okay, scratch for it. You can call me Mr. Scratch, but that name's already been taken by The Devil, I believe."

"I mean that you must hunt. Now, some animals hunt by night, and some animals hunt by day. To acquire money, because it is so hard to come by, you must hunt both night and day."

"And when do I sleep?" I inquire.

"As little as possible," says the bird. "And then play self-improvement tapes."

"May I ask you why you chose to show me this necklace?"

"Two reasons. Possibly three," says the bird, preening itself in an obnoxious manner. "First, don't turn up your nose at theft. It's as good a method as any. Used by all the major corporations and the U.S. government."

"I'm shocked," I gasp. "You are supposed to be sent to me from God."

"Remember the apple in the Garden of Eden," says the jay, "and draw your own conclusions."

"Second reason?"

"Second – you're not sure whether this necklace is real or fake, are you?"

"No, I'm –- "

"Pretense. Most of the money made in this country is based upon pretense. Even the money itself is pretending to stand for gold. Act as if! Pretend you already have money, and more will come to you. Pretend you have goods to sell, connections to be made, et cetera. Pretend you can help everybody, and they will help you. Very important."

"Is there a third reason?"

"For what?"

"For showing me the necklace."

"I didn't have to show it to you," snaps the bird, with what I could swear was a sneer. "You noticed it right away."

"Well, of course," I concur, "because of the – "

"Glitter," supplies the bird, cocking his head. "Glitz, Gleam, Glamor, Gloss, Glory -– Clothe yourself in everything beginning with GL and you will begin to acquire the secrets of attracting wealth – which is primarily based on attracting attention."

"What about Glum and Gloom?"

"There are exceptions to every rule."

The bird picks up the necklace in its beak, then puts it down again. "Notice the way I shine?" he asks, virtually strutting in front of me.

"When you stand in the sunlight and not the shadows," I reply.

"Dress to kill," the bird advises. "And don't hide in the shadows. People will respect you. One can never be too well dressed – for any occasion."

"I'll bear that in mind," I tell him.

"*Au revoir*," says the bird.

"You speak French?" I exclaim, aghast.

"I speak as many languages as possible," the jay says.

"But what does that have to do with –?"

"One must identify what people need and then find ways of meeting that need," says the bird. "One way to identify their needs is to speak to people in their own language."

"But I have no time to go back to school and – "

"Speaking of Time," says the jaybird, "I've got to go now. You know what Time is."

"But you didn't tell me exactly how to make it. Money, I mean."

"Every which way you can," says the bird, and with what I'll swear is a wink, he flies away.

* * *

I decided that a couple of fun ways to make money would be to sell stuff in flea markets and to give singles parties in my apartment. (Robbery was not an option for me, nor was becoming a glamour girl. The best thing about receiving advice, I find, is that you don't have to take all of it, only what works for you.) The part about identifying needs appealed to me. People need to buy things on the cheap, I figured, and they also need to meet kindred souls in this lonely, competitive city.

These moneymaking projects had several wonderful perquisites: They put me in contact with a variety of people, they required no major investment of capital, and they allowed me the time to continue working on my book. For a writer, Time certainly is Money.

CHAPTER THREE
THE BEAVER
(Writer's Block)

I had started writing a book and I was stuck. It had never happened to me before, but the task seemed so tremendous, so overwhelming. It was in a genre I'd never tried before, which was daunting enough – but what seemed even more overwhelming was the prospect of marketing it. I found myself willing to do any stupid task – getting my watch repaired, cooking huge meals in advance and storing them in the freezer, even cleaning the house – anything to avoid finishing the darn thing. I needed help.

* * *

So I make my mind a blank and go in my imagination to that favorite spot in the woods, next to a brook, where I soon find myself watching a beaver swim energetically back and forth from the edge of the water to the center of the brook. He is building a dam.

"Hallo!" I call to him.

"Hallo, yourself!" he calls back, and keeps on working.

"Could I speak to you for a few minutes?" I ask.

"Certainly," the beaver yells back. "But I might not have the time to answer you!"

"If you could only spare me a tiny bit of your time, I'd be extremely grateful," I say. "I just have one simple question." The beaver swims to shore near me, shakes himself off, and sits at attention.

"What, what, what?" he asks.

"Do you know why you were sent here?" I ask.

"You call that an easy question?" the beaver replies.

"No, I don't mean in general, I mean right now."

"I suppose it's because they think I'm eager," says the beaver. "Eager, eager, eager."

"Yes, I think that's it," I tell him. "I want to become an eager beaver myself, but lately I've been sluggish and despondent and – and – how do you do it?"

"Do what?"

"Be eager?"

"I'm not," the beaver informs me. "I just do what I have to do."

"Yes," I say, "But I can't seem to. You see, I have writer's block."

"Writer's block? What kind of wood is that made of?"

"It's not made of wood at all," I explain. "It just means I'm stuck, and I can't go on writing."

The beaver lets go with a loud guffaw. "Ridiculous!" he sputters.

"It's not at all ridiculous," I pout. "I can't seem to write, and when I don't write, I get depressed, and when I get depressed, I get sick. And I believe you have been sent here to heal me."

"Writer's block!" The beaver seems about to go into another paroxysm of laughter, but I stare at him so morosely he stops. "Have you ever heard of lumberjack's block? Or how about plumber's block? Or have you ever heard a carpenter complain of carpenter's block?"

"No," I reply. "Except for an actual piece of wood."

"Exactly. I happen to be a carpenter by trade. Do you ever see me moping about, complaining 'I don't feel like cutting any sticks today'?"

"You're a carpenter?" I echo. "I thought you were an architect."

"The plans have already been made in advance. I just carry them out," the beaver says. "Carry them out, carry them in, carry them off." I store this thought in my mind, for perhaps the plans for my book are also there somewhere, and what I need is to consult with The Architect. But the beaver is in a hurry, and there's no time for theological explorations right now.

"So you're telling me the main thing is just to get down to work," I say with a grimace . "Easier said than done."

"What sort of project are you building?" the beaver inquires.

"It's a book."

Again, my toothy friend falls apart laughing. "Ridiculous!" he shouts again. "You can't make a brook! The rain does that!"

"Not a brook, a book!" I correct him. I suspect he has water in his ears.

"Well, I don't know anything about such things, so I can't help you," the beaver says.

"It's very big," I tell him. "So big I don't know how to begin to tackle it."

"How about tackling it one twig at a time?" I stare at him in amazement. Of course, that's it! Cut the food on your plate into bite-size pieces! "I'd be mightily befuddled, I suppose, if I had to build a whole damn dam all at once," the beaver continues. "By the way, what's a book made of?"

"Paper," I tell him.

"Paper? Paper? Ridiculous! Paper is easy! But it won't hold much."

"Well, there's a bit more to it than that," I try to explain. "You have to put things on the paper."

"Things? Things? What sort of things?"

"Thoughts, feelings – that's where I get bogged down."

"Nothing ever bogs me down," the beaver says. "Unless I bog myself down. Stay under water just for the fun of it."

"Are you implying that I'm getting some sort of perverse pleasure from –?"

"I never imply," the beaver says. "Plywood's much too flimsy. It's the whole tree or nothing."

We seem to be having cultural differences. I change the subject. "Don't you ever get scared?" I ask him.

"Oh, yes. Then I just slap the water with my tail, and the other beavers come running."

"I could, I suppose, ask some friends to read what I've got so far – " I muse.

"Is it bigger than a beaver dam?" the creature wants to know.

"Is what bigger than a beaver dam?"

"This engineering project you're working on. This book thing."

"I don't know," I reply. "I have no idea how big a beaver dam is."

"I never know either," the beaver confesses, "Until after it's done."

"Don't you ever feel like not building a dam at all?" I ask.

"Sure," the beaver says. "On days like that I might work on building a lodge. Or a canal. I guess you might say I've always got some project I'm working on. Cutting down little trees, chopping them up into twigs, putting the twigs together with mud – "

"I see what you're saying. It's important to keep on perfecting your craft."

"No, I don't do rafts. Maybe someday, but not right now."

"Not raft," I correct him. "Craft. The art of constructing whatever it is you construct."

"Yes, yes, it is an art. And as with any art, the more you work at it, the better you get. When I was just a little shaver, for example, I couldn't even tell one tree from another."

"But how do you choose – "

"Which tree?" the beaver reads my mind. "Whichever it's easiest to sink your teeth into."

"Ah."

"And if you don't have enough material, you better go find some more. You might be looking in the wrong place."

"Mmmm."

"We collect material all the time, and store it in our lodges. You never know when you might run across a juicy tidbit."

"Thank you," I say. "You've been extremely helpful. I'll let you get back to your construction crew."

"Don't have one," the beaver says. "I'm an independent contractor. If I don't finish the job, nobody else will."

"Chop, chop!" I grin at him.

"I'll let you get back to your Writer's Block!" he grins, and dives back into the water.

"Ridiculous!" I call after him. "There's no such thing!"

CHAPTER FOUR
THE BEE
(Fame and Success)

There's no sense in living in New York City, I figured, unless you're wealthy and at the top of your field. But there I was, in the belly of the beast, the heart of the theatre and publishing industries, feeling like "the real nowhere man" in the Beatles song. Amid the subway roar I retreated to the woods to ask for help in chasing that elusive goddess, Fame.

* * *

A large yellowjacket buzzes around my head and addresses me in Black English:

"It be eazzy, sugar, but yet and still, it ain't eazzy."

"What's that supposed to mean?" I ask.

"Eazzy if you hustle your bustle like me, but not eazzy if you are lazy."

"Lazy? Who, me? No one has ever accused me of that before!"

The bee turns up a tiny radio and begins to click her feet in time to the rhythm. It's a rap song with lyrics that go something like: "If you want satisfaction, you gotta swing into action; think about addition and not subtraction; you want to meet the elite, you gotta move your feet! Get out on the street and give the world something sweet!" The bass is hurting my eardrums.

"Would you mind turning your radio down?" I request.

"You on my turf now, baby," she replies. "You listen to *my* music!" She then instructs me to come follow her. I can tell from her imperious tone that she is a Queen Bee, so I obey.

The hive is abuzz with her servants. She quotes to me from Lewis Carroll: "How doth the little busy bee improve each shining hour?"

"Well, how does she?" I ask.

"*Zahring*," says the bee (My Aunt Viola used to call me that – it means "darling" in German) – "we use the law of averages."

I ponder that for a moment and then ask, "How can I–?"

"We don't go to one or two flowers in search of pollen, you know," explains the bee. "If we did, baby, I wouldn't have much of a kingdom."

"Many flowers," I nod.

"Many, many, <u>many</u> flowers," replies the bee. "As many as you can find in twenty-four hours!"

"Is that it?" I ask.

"Patience, underling," the bee reprimands. "Observe!" She motions me to look around at the bustling hive.

"They work together," I note.

"And you are trying to win all your battles all alone," observes the bee. "No wonder you have headaches."

"How did you know?" I ask, then remember who sent her to me. "But I don't have a team like yours," I protest.

"I wasn't born with one either," says the Queen.

"Then how –?"

"Communication," says the bee, rubbing her feet together. She then begins whizzing around in what can only be described as a breakdance.

"Communication through entertainment?" I guess.

"Exactly. When you gots nothing, that's the time to act like you really got something. And the main thing you got is your own self – so make the most of it."

"My own self?"

"The way you use your voice, the way you walk, the way you make an entrance into a room. It's all a performance, girl. You gotta have z-z-z-zing!"

"I'd have to go to acting school."

"Naw, all you'd have to do is lighten up, zahring. It's called acting as if."

"As if what?"

"As if you already have what you want. Look at me," she says. "I wear this jazzy, snazzy yeller coat, which I couldn't afford when I got it – but it brought me so many admirers it was worth the investment. That's what I mean. Act as if."

I look at her. "It is a nice jacket," I comment.

"Oh, honey," groans the queen. "This fur jacket ain't <u>nice</u> at all. It's loud and it's crude, but it draws attention and it makes me stand out in a crowd, and that's what I want. Because the secret is, girl, you got to go to them, but you got to make them think they's coming to you!" She appraises me for a moment and then says, "Another thing, child. You got to lose that sweater."

"What's wrong with it?"

"Just about everything. The color don't do a thing for you, it makes you invisible. Me, I like bright color. Make folks stand up and take notice."

"But I'm not sure that's me," I say defensively.

"Well, what <u>is</u> you?" she challenges. "What is your – like they say – persona?"

"I don't know," I confess. "I've never thought about it."

"Well, if you don't got a persona, you be persona non grata,"

"Listen," I say, uncomfortable with so many home truths all at once, "I don't want to take you away from your honeymaking. I know you must be very busy, being a bee and all."

"I don't make the honey, honey," the queen says haughtily. "I delegate responsibility."

I'm afraid I've hurt her feelings, so I ask her timidly, "Then, what is your role, precisely?"

"Me? I'm a sex object," she whispers, and she rolls her gigantic eyes raffishly. "They willing to be drones because I'm gorgeous and they worship me."

"Well, I'm a writer, you see," I tell her, "and I tend to be rather shy."

"Get over it," the queen says. "You gotta go to the flowers, baby. The flowers ain't gonna come to you." As if to illustrate, she flies around in a circle and comes back to me. We go along in silence for a few moments, the bee just stopping to call my attention to the beautiful colors of the wildflowers. Just before we reach the place where we started from, the bee says, "Do you know what surprises and amuses me about you, Miz. Human?"

"No, what?" I ask, slightly taken aback.

"You have not even asked me once about my very special thing, I mean my sting."

"I was afraid of offending you; I was just trying to be nice," I apologize.

"There you go with that <u>nice</u> again," says the bee. "You gonna nice your way into the poorhouse, and dig yourself a nice little grave."

"What do you want me to do – become nasty and aggressive?"

"Hey, chill out, doll. You'll notice I don't go around stinging people for no good reason."

"That would be self-destructive," I comment.

"But neither do I let folks put me down or mess with me. God gave us all stingers for a reason. So, use yours when it's necessary. Don't be so damn nice when it's not appropriate. You have obviously been taking lessons from flies instead of bees."

"Flies?" I repeat, "I don't know any flies."

"Just as well," says the bee. "All flies know how to do is make pests of themselves. But nobody takes them seriously. Bees, on the other hand –"

"Carry with them the Death Penalty."

"Oh, baby, I don't want to kill nobody. I jest want 'em to know that I could make 'em mighty uncomfortable unless they do right by me. When they talking to you, they got to feel they in the presence of a queen!"

"A queen," I reiterate. "I wonder how that would feel."

"Power scares you, don't it?" the bee jeers as a challenge. "And I think I know why."

"My parents were the power figures in my family," I tell her. "I was – "

"Invisible?" I nod. "Well, they be gone now," she reminds me. "So you can have all the power and visibility you want. But y'know, there's good power and bad power. I use mine for making honey. Ain't nothin' wrong with that."

"About this flying business," I begin.

"Oh, so you want to fly, now, too?" she laughs.

"Metaphorically speaking," I shrug, "I want to rise above my present circumstances. I want to be a celebrity, like you."

"First learn to walk," instructs the bee. "First things first."

"Oh, yes," I say, "I've heard that expression."

"I bet you've heard a heap of expressions," says the bee. "But your trouble is you don't put them into a pattern."

"A pattern?"

"I go for hexagons, myself," muses the bee. "I'm not sure why. They just seem to suit me. I'm not saying hexagons are necessarily for you –"

"Just that I should try to find a pattern."

"Mmm. Think back on three success experiences you've had. Times you connected with people. Times you did make a sale. What did all them happenings have in common?"

"Let's see," I frown. "There's my son, a *wunderkind,* my greatest creation. And the children's show I wrote in three weeks and had produced. And the poetry I've gotten published. What they all had in common, I guess, was that they came so easily to me."

"Interesting," the bee says. "Seems like Fame and Success are not things you chase after; they're by-products of doing whatever work you find easy and others find difficult."

I confess to her about turning off the TV when I see a successful person in my field, I'm so overcome with jealousy. And recently walking out on a book-signing of a friend of mine.

"They don't call it the Green-Eyed Monster for nothing, babe. It's a mighty waste of energy."

"How's that?"

"Do you think that famous and successful person is sitting around thinking about you?"

"Of course not," I reply.

"Okay, what do they be doing?"

"Perfecting their craft," I answer. "Doing their work. Getting out and meeting people."

"That's right," she encourages me. "They be doing their thing. As best as they can. No, what you should be doing when you meet a person more successful than you is hook up with them. Ask 'em for help in getting work or in meeting the people you want to meet."

"Oh, do you think they would actually help me?"

"You never know 'till you try," she says. "They might just want a protégé."

We have reached the large oak tree where I like to sit when visiting the glade. The bee whispers, "*Auf wiedersehen, zahring.* I have a tryst in five minutes. But let me put this bee in your bonnet: Stay busy. The antidote for Depression is Action." And away she zooms, making a bee-line for her next engagement.

CHAPTER FIVE
THE CAMEL
(Handling Stress)

Between the demands of my teaching job, my attempts to write and to market my writing, and the frenetic stimulations of a New York social life, I'd been running around like a lunatic and found myself totally stressed out. This worried me, because the last time I came under tremendous stress, I got breast cancer, and I didn't want that to happen again. Practicing the relaxation techniques I learned at a Buddhist ashram, I sat in the sacred sanctuary I'd created in my home, took deep breaths, and tried to return in my mind to my favorite sylvan place.

* * *

Instead, I find myself in a desert.

"Hey, wait a minute," I say to myself. "This is not my kind of place. I am definitely not the desert type. I am more woods, or maybe lakes. Deserts and me – nah. I get sunburned too easily, and the sand gets in my toes and itches, and – "

But a great booming voice says, "Stay there."

The sun is feeling kindly, comfortable and warm, and I feel lazy and unwilling to move, so I acquiesce. The next thing I know, I'm riding on a camel. The ride is bumpy and pleasantly rollicking. I put my face next to the camel's, and say, "What can you teach me?"

"What do you wish to know?" the camel asks. His is the booming voice I heard before.

"I think I've been working too hard, I'm under a lot of stress, and I'm afraid I'm going to get cancer again and maybe die."

The camel laughs a snorting sort of laugh, stops, kneels, and allows me to dismount. "My dear," he says, resting on his knobby knees, "If hard work gave a person cancer, then I and all the other beasts of burden would have been dead and buried long ago! Don't you know what Stress is?" The dromedary does not wait for my reply. "If you are pulling a rope from both ends in opposite directions – or applying pressure and force to a body that's resistant and pushing back – a tension occurs, and that tension is called Stress."

"So, you mean that my stress is caused by – "

"Working very hard at what you don't want to do." I fill him in on all the important things I really must attend to. "And when," he asks me, "Do you give yourself time to daydream?"

"Excuse me?"

"I can teach you three things," the camel drawls. "First, build up your reserves!"

"What kind of reserves?" I ask. "Do you mean money?"

"That, too," the camel says, sleepily, as if money doesn't much matter to him one way or the other. I guess he meant inner reserves, the way he stores water, and that he was advising me to accumulate skills, preserve my strength and my health.

"Do you think we're in for a drought?" I ask.

"We're always in for a drought," he responds. "In one way or another. So you need to provide yourself with the physical, mental, and emotional wherewithal to withstand the slack periods. That's where daydreams come in. They help us visualize our goals."

"But how – ?"

"Don't keep looking for the oasis," the camel says. "Become an oasis." He sighs, and then nods off completely. I pace up and down thinking about what I'm spending my energies on unnecessarily. I become hot and sweaty and terribly thirsty. There seems to be no water around for miles, and I'm afraid to go looking for some, fearing I might get lost and not find my way back. I am tempted to wake the camel up, but have no idea what an angry camel might act like. At last, the sun begins to descend and a cool breeze stirs the sand. The camel opens one eye, stretches, and yawns.

"Camel, camel, I've been waiting for you to wake up!" I cry. "I want to know what the second thing is!"

"Haven't you figured it out yourself?" the camel asks.

"No," I tell him. "I've been pacing up and down working up a sweat trying to guess what it could be."

"Oh, dear," the camel says. "I tried to provide you an example, but you paid no attention."

"What do you mean?" I ask. "An example of what?"

"Whenever the situation gets too hot," he says, "The thing to do is rest."

"Rest!" I fairly scream at him. "First the bee tells me to stay busy, and now you tell me I should rest! I wish you creatures would make up your mind!"

"Mmmm," the camel utters drowsily, peering at me from under his droopy eyes. "And that's the third thing."

"What is?"

"How do you think I have been able to carry so many people and packages on long journeys for so many centuries?"

"I don't know. How?"

"Balance," says the camel. "You need to achieve Balance."

"I, too, have many burdens I must carry," I argue.

"So do we all," the camel sighs. "But we must wait and listen for the winds. Then travel in the proper direction – and only when we are well prepared and when the conditions are right." He turns his head and nods at a knapsack he's been carrying.

"Refresh yourself," he suggests. I look inside, and there's a canteen of water for me. I take a long, delicious drink. Then I lie down next to the camel, and together we watch the stars come out in the night sky.

CHAPTER SIX
OWL AND RHINOCEROS
(A Head for Business)

I'm not making much at the weekend flea markets because I don't charge enough, and my singles parties are not a great source of revenue because I let all my friends come in free. My teaching salary doesn't support the kind of lifestyle I'd like to become accustomed to, but when I try to supplement my income with writing, I'm offered rock bottom payment for my articles and stories. I came out the financial loser in my divorce, so there's no alimony to fall back on, and we sold the house for much less than it was worth. The fact is, every time I've either bought or sold anything I seem to have lost money on the deal. "Why am I such an underearner?" I asked, as I went in my mind to a shady spot at the edge of a river.

* * *

I stare at the river for awhile, trying to recall the words to "Men may come and men may go, but I go on forever," when an owl appears on the branch of a tree, perching in such a way that I have to look up at him.

"I need to know how to become a nabob," I tell the owl.

"Who, you?" the owl hoots.

"Yeah, me," I reply. "I know I've always conveyed the image of the scatterbrained artist. But this year I need money in order to travel and buy some new clothes. I'd like to run my writing career more like a profession than a hobby, but I'm afaid I don't have much of a head for business. I could use some advice."

The owl swoops down and sits nearer to me, on a fallen log directly in view.

"Have you tried consulting the American Association for Retired Persons?" he asks. "They have business execs who can tell you how to keep records and draw up a marketing plan. You do keep records, don't you?"

"Well, I – "

The owl stares at me with big round eyes that remind me of my mother's. She was an excellent businessperson. She ran her own secretarial agency and enjoyed keeping spreadsheets. I wish I had paid more attention to the one thing she did have to offer me, instead of focusing on what she could not give me.

"I don't mean stuff like how to keep the books," I say. "I can read up on that later. I need to know what personality changes I must undergo in order to be taken seriously as a businessperson."

"Not putting off details until later might be one," the owl says. He looks around with his amazing capacity to turn his head in almost a 360-degree arc. "Why don't I introduce you to the rhinoceros. He's no Einstein, mind you, but he does know how to get things done."

"Wait a minute," I frown. "I thought this was a woods. Rhinoceroses are located in river valleys, primarily in Africa and Asia."

"We have contacts everywhere," the owl boasts. "Wait here." I wait, staring at the river in front of me. In a few minutes, I witness the amazing sight of a rhinoceros floating towards me down the river, with an owl on its back. The rhino is wearing an explorer's safari hat on its head.

"Here he is," the owl whispers, as the rhino shakes off droplets of water and lumbers towards me. "Frame your questions carefully," the owl suggests. "He's very jealous of his time."

"Mr. Rhino – " I begin.

"Louder," the owl coaches. "He's slightly hard of hearing.

"Really? But I thought rhinoceroses had excellent hearing."

"They do, but this one got in a fight with a poacher who wanted to grind up his horn to make aphrodisiacs. The poacher hit our friend on the head, and his hearing has never been the same since. But he's a survivor. That's why I want you to meet him."

"Are you sure he'll want to speak to me? Won't he want to exact some sort of revenge on two legged creatures such as myself?"

"He already has," the owl says. "He derailed a train in Nigeria. He's much calmer now. And he does love to be interviewed. Go ahead. He's all yours. I'll wait in the tree."

"Mr. Rhino," I begin again, only louder, and enunciating clearly. "I'd like to become better at handling my finances. I might even like to start my own business. But I, but I –"

"But you can never bring yourself to mention the subject of money," the rhino guesses. He has a faint British accent. "You consider it impolite."

"Well, it is rather embarrassing."

"Money is only embarrassing if you don't have enough of it," the rhino quips.

"You must be a fan of Oscar Wilde," I remark.

"Don't know him," the rhino snorts. "Just how wild was he?"

"Never mind," I say. "I'd like you to tell me what makes a good businessperson."

"Observe your interlocutor," says the rhino. "It's rather obvious."

"Thick skin," I note.

"Very. I never take rejection personally. I suggest you pay no attention to rejection at all; just go after what you want. And the main thing you want is to stay afloat, isn't it?"

"Yes, of course."

"Then you have to respect money. You have to take money seriously. Because money is what keeps you afloat. Above all – don't ever work for nothing, set your fees and method of payment right at the outset, and don't smile when you tell people your terms."

"And what are your terms?"

"I've agreed to this consultation on a contingency basis. I want fifty percent of your first month's profits and a very nice fish."

"That would be agreeable with me," I tell him.

"You gave in too soon," he chides me. "You should have haggled a bit. It's expected. Very well, then. Observe me, and tell me what you see." He spins around slowly, like a wobbly top just winding down, and then stops, posing in profile.

"The horn."

"Quite."

"As in tooting your own?"

"Precisely. If you don't, nobody will. It's also a weapon."

"I'm not much of a fighter," I sigh.

"Neither am I," the rhinoceros confesses. "But I try to give the impression that I am. That way nasty animals don't bother me, and if they do, I raise a terrible rumpus and they usually back down in terror."

"That's good," I say dubiously, "But I can't grow a horn."

"What's the equivalent?" the rhino asks Socratically.

"A no-nonsense approach, I suppose."

"What's that?" the rhino shouts. He could use an ear-horn.

"A no-nonsense approach!" I yell, a few decibels louder. He jumps.

"You scared me half to death," he admits.

"I didn't mean to. I'm sorry," I apologize.

"Never apologize," the rhino says. "You're supposed to scare people at first. That's the whole idea. Now, what else do you notice?"

"Well," I hesitate. "I hope you're not offended by this — "

"I told you not to worry about my feelings," the rhino reminds me. He points to his thick skin.

"Well, I guess you know," I posit tentatively, "You're not terribly good-looking."

"Don't care, don't even try to be," the rhino shrugs. "I'm not concerned with pleasing people. I'm interested in getting results and making scads of money. I suppose you've noticed my wrinkles." I nod. "That's because I'm always looking for a new wrinkle, a new scheme. It's lots of fun. Go on."

"Go on?"

"You haven't finished my description. What else do you see?"

"Protective coloring?"

"Muddy, to be exact. I don't mind getting down and dirty, if it's what the job requires. Got to get your feet wet. Jump in. Don't hesitate too long; someone else will beat you to the punch.

28

Mistakes can be corrected after awhile. Trust your own judgment."

"Do you always speak in such short sentences?" I can't help inquiring.

"Not an animal of many words. An animal of action."

"What do you do, mostly?" I ask.

"Charge things, of course," he says.

"Oh, I can do that," I say.

"Can you?" he challenges me. If a rhinoceros had eyebrows, he would raise them. I realize I have a difficult time borrowing, running up credit, "charging things."

"You'll have to learn how to use other people's money," he counsels. I gulp at this. Some people have trouble saving; I have trouble spending. "Now, let me ask you some questions," the rhino says. He sits down and polishes his horn with a large leaf. "What personal characteristics do you have that would make you good in business? Your assets, as it were."

I list them for him: "I'm outgoing, courageous, responsible, perseverant – "

"Good!" he cries. "Build on those! The rest will take care of itself. You'll learn as you go along. If you are willing to profit by your mistakes. And now," he says, "Would you like to hear me play something?"

"On what?" I ask. Musical talent in a rhinoceros is the last thing I'd expected.

"The horn, of course," he replies. "Any requests?"

"Anything you like," I say. "Whatever you do best." He then astounds me, not only by being able to play the horn at all, but by offering a fairly credible rendition of *Traumerei*. He pauses and sighs when he's done, and scratches his back on a tree.

"You may scratch your back on my tree, if you like," he offers.

"Your tree?"

"Myself and the rest of the herd – more or less own an entire section of the river. It's our turf, if you will. We have something no one else has, and that they need."

"You didn't mention the herd."

"Didn't I? What an oversight! Deucedly important. Couldn't operate without the others!"

"Where do you get the others?"

"Family, mostly," says the rhino. "Best way. If not family, then close friends. Creatures who have proven they are worthy of Trust. And speaking of Trust, I've changed my mind about something. Instead of the percentage deal on your profits, which at this point I'm not sure you're actually going to make, I would like you to edit the book I'm writing."

"Book!" I cry. "I had no idea! What's it about?"

"It's called *My Uncle, the Unicorn*. They say to write about what you know."

"Fascinating title," I flatter him scandalously, but it's been my experience that writers are terribly vain. "But aren't unicorns, I mean, nonexistent, er, that is, they exist, but only in fantasy."

"Rather," agrees the rhino with enthusiasm.

"Then your book is primarily a study of the difference between...."

"Reality and illusion. Quite. And if you are to succeed in business, you'd better make that your perpetual study as well."

"That's not easy," I comment.

"I should say not!" the rhinoceros exclaims. "Nothing worthwhile is, you know. Did I mention hard work, keeping up with your field? Reading everything you can on your subject of expertise? I should have. Well, what do you say? Will you help me with the editing?"

"I'd be happy to," I assure him. I name an outlandishly high fee.

"I say, but you learn fast!" the rhino congratulates me. And he takes out from another fold in his hide a piece of paper and a pen, and forthwith draws up a contract. "Get it in writing, that's my motto. One of them, anyway." After we both sign copies of the document, the rhino astonishes me by tearing his up. "I haven't written a book at all," he tells me. "I was only testing you. I'll call you next week," he says. "We can do lunch. Toodle-ooo." And he waddles into the water.

CHAPTER SEVEN
THE RAT
(Leaving a Sinking Ship)

After my car was stolen for the sixth time, the final time returned to me with a totally demolished engine, and after an attempted burglary in my Brooklyn apartment, I began thinking I might want to leave New York City. But the prospect of moving was scary. I'd lived in New York my entire life. I remained there for the Culture, which I couldn't afford, and for the brilliant and successful people, who never phoned me to go anywhere. I was afraid to leave because my friends were there – friends who wanted to charge me money any time I asked for a favor. Besides, if I did leave New York, where could I go?

I meditated on "Where Shall I Go?" and was given the words "South Fallsburg, New York." I looked this place up on a map and found it was in the Catskills. I'd spent several summers in the Catskills as a child, but could see no good reason to move there. Several days later I received a call from a friend named Margie, who asked me if I wanted to go with her to an ashram. She had found a wonderful place that charged only twenty-five dollars for the weekend and provided inexpensive bus transportation from the city.

"Where is it?' I asked.

"In South Fallsburg, New York," she replied. I felt that this piece of Synchronicity was too remarkable to ignore, and went with her to the ashram the following weekend.

The first evening, I was seated next to a dharma teacher at a savory dinner of beef stew (which I learned was actually made of tofu) and proceeded to tell him my tale of woe: I had been the victim of an intended robbery. I'd thought my apartment was safe, since it was on the fourth floor of an apartment building. So I'd only invested in bars for the window that faced the fire escape. But the criminal had stretched a plank of wood no more than six inches wide from the fire escape to an open unbarred window, and walked like a tightrope dancer several hundred feet above the ground, to enter my apartment. He heard me talking to friends in another room, and went back the same way he had come. But I could still see his dirty fingerprints on the windowsill, and each time I looked at them, I shook with fear.

"That poor fellow," the dharma teacher said.

"What?" I cried. "You have sympathy with the thief and not with me?"

"How desperate he must have been, how impoverished, to take such a tremendous risk."

"But don't you see how frightened I am?" I argued. "I don't want to keep living in such fear!"

"Then don't," the dharma teacher smiled. He invited me to come with him to the chanting after dinner.

At first the constant chanting of "Om Namayah Shivaya" amused me. Then I decided to try it, and found that the physical resonances of the chant cleaned out both my body and my mind and made it possible to enter deeper states of meditation. I got down on my knees and asked "Shall I leave New York?"

* * *

I am visited by – of all creatures – an alert and whisker-twitching rat. My first tendency is to scream and run. I've always been a bit squeamish about rodents of all descriptions, since I'd heard that they carry disease, including rabies and bubonic plague.

"Don't a-you worry," the rat says, in an unmistakable Italian accent. "I am not going to bite you."

"Are you sure?" I ask.

"Sure I'm sure," the rat asserts. "First of all, I am only a dream. And secondly I am here, as all dreams are here, to help you."

"What?" I exclaim. "They send me a rat to help me decide whether or not to move?"

"Why not?" is the rat's rejoinder. "I do get around, you know. My people discovered America."

"I always thought Christopher Columbus did that," I sneer disdainfully.

"Ha!" sniffs the rat. "That's because humans write the history books. They try to make themselves look like the big heroes. Do you want me to tell you what really happened?"

"Please."

The rat informs me that Christopher Columbus, after mucking about in the Sargasso Sea, became incredibly seasick and also depressed, and spent most of his time in his cabin. An experienced old tar of a rat organized a mutiny, and the rodents took over the wheel.

"You mean he didn't say 'Sail on, sail on, sail on and on'?" I cry in astonishment.

"Not exactly," the rat smiles knowingly. "What he actually said was 'Ceylon, Ceylon, where the hell is Ceylon?'"

"Why are you telling me this?" I say to the rat.

"You seem to require credentials," the rat says with a shrug. "I assure you, I have a long history as a voyager and a cartographer."

"If you discovered America, why isn't it called 'Ratland'?" I challenge him.

"That is precisely what we do call it," said the rat. "But very few speak our language."

"Well, big deal," I say, still finding it difficult to overcome my repulsion for this creature. "If you didn't discover America, somebody else would have. If that's your only claim to fame – "

"But it is not," the rat said. "I believe you have a problem. And when you have a problem, you should go to an expert."

"Oh? And exactly what is your particular brand of expertise?"

"Knowing when to abandon a sinking ship," says the rat. Now it was my turn to perk up my ears.

"Do you think New York City is a sinking ship?"

"Maybe for you it is," the rat replies.

"Look," I say. "Whether you know it or not, rats have a certain reputation. They're known as traitors, as quitters, as betrayers of their country!"

"Be that as it may," the rat says, "Sometimes there comes a time when it is healthier to go than to stay. It is for you to decide when that time is."

"I'm not a quitter," I say proudly.

"Then you are a fool," shrugs the rat.

"I beg your pardon?"

"Would you call Moses a quitter?" the rat counters. "He felt the time had come to gather up his people and depart from Egypt."

"Well, yes, but – "

"And the pioneers who in their covered wagons crossed America?"

"Well, they had to – "

"And the European Jews who in the Thirties fled the Nazis?"

"Oh, things are not that bad," I laugh.

"Not yet," the rat says, and begins filing his fingernails.

"Would you like some cheese?" I offer. I'm beginning to get interested in this conversation.

"What kind is it?" he inquires.

"You can have anything you like," I say. "After all, this is a dream."

"In that case," the rat says, "I'll have a chunk of Gorgonzola."

I produce a tray of cheese and crackers, and the rat surprises me by tying a cloth napkin around his neck, so as not to get crumbs on his coat.

"Do you mind if I ask you something?" I say.

"That's what I'm here for, evidently," the rat says.

"How do you know exactly when to leave the sinking ship?"

"Ah," says the rat. "Now we're getting down to business." I look into his eyes, which are not as beady as I first thought, and actually appear to be quite intelligent. He stretches out like a pasha at a Turkish banquet. "It is a question of comfort," he says.

"Comfort?"

"Yes. We are not comfortable getting drowned."

"I don't think anybody is," I say.

"So we make a thorough appraisal of the situation, and determine whether it is likely we shall or shall not be drowned if we remain."

"I sometimes feel I'm drowning in New York," I admit.

"You mustn't wait until you are drowning," the rat says. "By then it's too late."

"But if I did leave," I frown. "Where would I go?"

"Again, I repeat, wherever you are most comfortable."

"But I'm not sure – "

"Then you must meditate on it again one time." The rat gets up, smoothes himself out, and tells me he has to get back to his pack. "You may call on me again, if you wish," he says.

The next day, I enter into meditation again and find myself driving down a canopied road. There are great oak trees, with hanging moss making a beautiful tunnel. Also lining the road are Southern mansions. But they are lived in, I notice, because I can see bicycles on the front lawn. I realize I am in Florida, but all I know of Florida is postcards I have seen of Miami Beach.

"This can't be Florida," I say to Whoever Gives Us Dreams. "Florida has palm trees."

"No, my dear," says the Dream Master. "We have oaks and pines. This is Tallahassee."

Until this point, I have never heard of Tallahassee. I make a visit to the library at the ashram, and find a book called "Welcome to Florida." There I am amazed to learn that the city is the state capitol and the home of an excellent university. But what I read next startles me. "The city is known for its canopied roads and historic Southern mansions."

I decide I must talk to the rat again.

I go into a darkened prayer room, bow before a sculpture of the Buddha, and take such deep breaths I am dizzy. I request another visit with my pointy-nosed guide, and he enters my consciousness.

"I have been told to go to Tallahassee, Florida," I announce to him.

"Yes, what about it?" he asks.

"I don't know anybody there," I say.

"There are bound to be people there," the rat says. "It is not a desert. And probably some of residents will become your friends."

"But why Tallahassee?" I wonder. "What does it have to offer me?"

"What do you have to offer them?" The rat was obviously borrowing a page from the dharma teacher's book, by reversing my assumptions.

"I don't know," I sigh. "I don't know anything about the place."

"'Know thyself,' as one of my relatives once said."

"Come on, now," I contradicted. "That saying was written on the Delphic oracle."

"And who do you think wrote it there?" the rat retorted.

"I don't want to argue with you," I said. "I just want to know how I'm going to make this huge decision!"

"How about accumulating some facts? They never hurt when making any decision."

"I guess I'm just afraid of Change. Of facing the Unknown."

"But you do it every day," the rat says. "Nobody ever knows what's going to happen, from one moment to the next."

"Pardon me," I inquire, "But are you a Buddhist?"

"I do not answer personal questions," the rat says diffidently. "I will inform you, however, that I am a mystic, and believe there is a spirit in the universe which wants us to find balance."

"Do you think that Spirit, or whatever it is, will help me make this gigantic move?"

"Not unless you are willing to take action," the rat says. "The spirit may move you, but you've got to do the packing."

I ponder this a moment.

"What if I don't like it there?" I ask.

"You can always come back. There's only one decision that's totally irreversible. When you die, you die."

"I could try it out for a little while," I suggest.

"Yes, you could," the rat says. "See it not as a risk, but as an adventure!"

"Perhaps I could go there on a little vacation – "

"It is not impossible," the rat says. "Unless you are one of those dreadful humans who never takes a vacation."

"If I do like it, I could sublet my apartment. Perhaps even make some money on it, since the cost of living will no doubt be cheaper down there."

"There you go," said the rat. "You seem perkier already."

"I don't know what's gotten into me," I say, grinning from ear to ear.

"I do," says the rat.

"The spirit?"

I take a few more deep breaths. When I open my eyes, the rat is gone.

* * *

I came down to Tallahassee for a month to try it out. When I drove down the beautiful canopied roads lined with oaks laden with Spanish moss, and saw the real Southern mansions that I had witnessed in my vision, I felt that I belonged here. I bought a little house with a garden, rented my New York apartment, packed up the possessions I had thought were tying me down, and moved.

I found the cost of living to be half what it was in The Big Apple; the people were warm and friendly, and I was able to be my creative self in a nurturing environment. Thank you, Mr. Rat, for helping me make the transition!

CHAPTER EIGHT
THE RED ANT
(Adjusting to New Surroundings)

For the first couple of months after I arrived in Tallahassee, I thought I'd landed smack in the middle of Paradise. Here was so much natural beauty – great live oak trees, draped with lacy Spanish moss, azaleas and magnolias in magnificent profusion. A lake in the middle of town, with ducks and geese and herons and anhinga. Temperate weather, with comforting sun. And the people were warm and friendly and gracious. The traffic, compared to the snarls and gridlock of metropolis, was a breeze; I could get anywhere in town in ten minutes, so my days seemed richer and fuller, less of a hassle. There did not seem to be any crime to speak of. I was wrong, of course. I relaxed, which was what I needed to do. But I relaxed too much.

The first stupid thing I did was this: I had bought a house on the south side of town, for one-quarter of the price an equivalent house would have been in New York. It was cute and charming and had three bedrooms, a front lawn with a garden, and a huge backyard surrounded by shady trees. "Ah, I'm practically in the country!" this city girl said, and the first month I was there, I lay down on the grass in my back yard to catch some rays. I arose around fifteen minutes later, stung all over my legs and arms by red ants. It was an itchy, painful reminder that problems are everywhere. There would be different problems here from the ones in New York, but problems there would definitely be.

I also was acting under erroneous assumptions about crime. No muggers followed me home as they had done in Brooklyn, but I left my car doors open as the vehicle sat overnight in the driveway, and a bunch of teenagers came and sat inside smoking cigarettes and stabbing the butts out on my upholstery, leaving burn holes all over the car. I was so ashamed of my stupidity in leaving the car doors open, I never got the upholstery repaired.

Another time, I left the house on a Sunday night to have coffee with a friend, leaving the kitchen window open to air the fumes out after cleaning the oven. When I returned, after only an hour, my front door was wide open. Someone had come in the kitchen window and cleaned out my entire stereo system and brand new TV. For weeks after that, I was afraid to go anywhere, thinking the robbers might return in my absence.

I'd also jumped to conclusions about the economic situation in the city of Tallahassee, drawing my inferences from perusing the Sunday pages of the *Tallahassee Democrat* for a few weeks and noting that it seemed to contain an abundance of employment opportunities. I found, however, when I began jobhunting, that jobs in state government were not easy to obtain, that my New York teaching credentials were not recognized and I'd have to start taking tests all over again to teach in the public school system, and that salaries here were abysmally low. I became so nervous about going through my savings that I started to develop psychosomatic pains in my stomach. Sometimes the pains were so bad, I could hardly walk.

Fearing I was about to become the same nervous wreck I had been when I lived in New York, I breathed deeply, concentrated on a bright white light, and went in my mind to my favorite meditation place in the woods.

* * *

Who should show up, staring at me with huge convex eyes from on top of a sandy hill, but a large red ant.

"Oh, it's you!" I mutter with annoyance.

"It is I," the ant responds. "You don't seem overjoyed to see me."

"Haven't you and your buddies given me enough trouble, causing me to be covered in calamine lotion for an entire week?"

"We just did it to teach you a lesson," the ant says.

"What lesson is that?"

"That there are problems everywhere you go."

"Yes, I believe I've noticed that."

"And we wanted you to ask yourself something."

"Ask myself what?"

"How do you handle problems?"

I sit down – on a tree stump, this time, not on the grass – and think about this a minute.

"Usually," I reply, "When a problem arises, I freak out for awhile. I panic. I go berserk."

"Why is that?" the ant asks.

"I'm not sure," I frown. "I think because my parents asked me to grow up too soon. I've always felt too young, too unprepared to handle what I needed to handle in life."

"I see," the ant says. "And what do you say to yourself during this freaking-out period?"

"It's usually something like, 'Oh my god, a problem! What will I do? I can't cope! I'll wind up a bag lady! I'll get sick and nobody will take care of me! I'll die a horrible death!'"

"Isn't that a bit of an extreme reaction?" the ant asks.

"Of course," I admit. "But you asked me what goes through my mind, and that's what I hear."

"Stinky thinking," the ant comments. "And then what?"

"Then I usually smoke a cigarette or two. Or, depending on the magnitude of the problem, a whole pack."

"Oh, that's a big help," the ant sniffs sarcastically.

"Look, I'm trying to be honest with you, you little creep," I snap at the ant, reverting to my New York method of conversation. "The least you can do is refrain from being so judgmental!"

"Fine," says the ant. "You panic, smoke, say stupid mantras to yourself. And then what?"

"Well, eventually, I begin to work out a plan of action."

"All by yourself?"

"Naturally, all by myself."

"Naturally?"

"Well, I can't ask other people to solve my problems for me."

"You've been seeing too many John Wayne movies."

"What?"

"The myth of the lonesome cowboy," the ant says. "A uniquely American phenomenon. The lonesome cowboy rides into town, fights the villain, and cleans up all the greed, corruption and violence all by himself."

"Isn't that the way heroes usually work?" I ask.

"Not in the real world," the ant says. "Especially not in my world."

"How do *you* solve problems, then?" I inquire.

"We do it together," the ant says. "Me and my co-workers, me and my friends. First, we share information. Then, we share ideas. Then, we share tasks. Then, we share the results."

"I don't like to ask for help," I tell the ant.

"Obviously," the ant says. "You didn't even go to a doctor for your ant bites, but decided to use calamine lotion. A doctor would have suggested how to relieve both the pain and the itching and would have cleared the whole thing up in a day with antibiotics. You're lucky you didn't get Lyme disease."

"There you go again!" I yell. "You're being critical!"

"Sorry," the ant says. "But you're supposed to be the creatures with the big brains. It's amazing how seldom you use them."

"Don't forget," I remind the ant, "that ants are social insects. I live in an anti-social culture."

"You can say that again," the ant says.

"I'd prefer not to," I grumble.

"And what do you suppose would happen if you did ask for help?"

"They'd probably say no."

"You're sure about that?"

"It's been my experience. In New York. People are too busy, too self-involved, to reach out and give of their time, their energy, their money."

"Well, Dorothy, you're not in New York any more," the ant observes. "And even in New York, I'll wager you could get help from people if you knew how to ask."

"I'm not used to it," I confess. "I don't know how."

"Well, you might start by getting rid of those negative mantras."

"Easier said than done," I protest.

"Yes," the ant sighs, "Force of habit is one of the most powerful forces in the world."

"You think I just say these things to myself out of force of habit?"

"Don't you?"

"I don't know. I never thought about it."

"Mmmm," the ant says. "That's why it's a habit. You do it without thinking. You may have to retrain yourself – to say positive mantras next time a problem arises."

"Positive mantras? Give me an example."

"Here's one I like," the ant says. "God loves me."

"Do ants believe in God?"

"We couldn't go about our business unless we did," the ant says. "Although our God may be different from your God. We believe there is a universal order, and that it is beneficent, that God wants to help us. Otherwise why would he put food in our path for us to nibble on and earth for us to build our homes? Why would he supply us with venom for self defense and a means of communication so we can live in harmony?"

"Well, just because I say something doesn't mean it's going to happen," I object.

"Ah," the ant contradicts me, "But I'm here to tell you it will. If you say it often enough, until you believe it, and it becomes a self-fulfilling prophecy."

"Another mantra, please," I request.

"I am a child of God," the ant replies. "Made in the image of God, with all the qualities of the creator."

"What does that mean?" I ask.

"It means that you deserve help when you ask for it," the ant says. "If someone denies you help, they have failed to see the worthiness in you. It is their insufficiency, not yours."

"That's a nice way of looking at it," I say. "But what do you do when the problem is really, really big?"

"All problems are really, really big," the ant says. "Or really, really small. Depending on how you look at them. My major problems would probably seem infinitesimal to you. Your major problems would probably seem trivial to an elephant, or a whale."

"You think I should keep things in perspective," I surmise.

"It might help," the ant shrugs. "But mostly you must realize that every problem has at least one solution."

"But how do you arrive at it?"

"Have you heard of the scientific method?" the ant asks.

"Yes, I've heard of it," I answer. "They told us about it in high school. You don't mean to tell me that insects use scientific method!"

"All the time," the ant replies. "Let's say the problem is that a large tree branch has fallen in the path, blocking the way to our food source."

"Okay, what do you do then?"

"Someone proposes a hypothetical solution. Let's say Anita Ant proposes that we climb over the branch. We try it out, experiment. We try climbing over the branch. It is too slippery, and we fall off. Then Annabelle Ant suggests we go around the branch. We try that. Another large object is in the way. That won't work. Then Andrea Ant puts forth the idea that we dig our way under the branch. We try that, and we succeed."

"You mean, you don't always do what your queen mandates you to do?" I ask.

"Oh, no, no, no! Frankly, the queen is just a glorified playgirl, a figurehead. We worker ants, we're the backbone of the society."

"And who are the soldier ants?"

"Oh, we worker ants are often conscripted into service," the pismire tells me. "And a fine lot of soldiers we'd be, if we panicked at every assault, the way you do."

"So how would your colony of worker ants handle my jobhunting problems?" I ask.

"Very badly," the ant replies. "You see, animals and insects have to do everything by trial and error. You humans are blessed in that you can hold many options, many alternative solutions in your head at the same time. You can try them out in your imagination. This gives you an overall picture far more advanced than ours. This is why you have Galileos and Einsteins, and we do not."

"Actually, it's the creative problems I do best with," I confide to the ant. "It's the stupid little everyday ones I have the most trouble with."

"It seems to me," said the ant, "that you don't have trouble with the problems at all. What you have trouble with is all the nonsense that goes on inside your head when you forget that the antidote to fear is action."

"That's good," I compliment him. "I like that. Your bits of wisdom almost compensate for the large number of welts you gave me."

"Welt," the ant muses, "is German for 'world.' What we have given you is a large number of worlds. And hopefully, a more enlightened *weltanschauung*."

"I'll work on the mantras," I say.

"You do that," the ant says. "And now, KYAKA!"

"What?"

"It stands for 'Keep your antennae keenly activated,'" the ant translates. "It's our salutation of goodbye."

* * * * *

The following week, I consulted my neighbors about forming a Neighborhood Watch, and meanwhile upped the coverage on my home insurance. I consulted with a minister about the frustrations of my job search, and she told me I was capable of creating my own job. Reaching out to several state departments and teaching institutions, I developed a course for teaching English to state workers.

I started taking tennis lessons, and made the association that when the ball comes at me, I have no time to say to myself, "Oh my god, here's the ball, what shall I do, I'll never be able to get it, I'll lose the game and be humiliated in my community forever!" As soon as the ball leaves my opponent's racket, I must swing into action, quickly examining my choices on how to best connect – forehand, backhand, overhead, volley – "It's only a game!" I tell myself. And, come to think of it, so is life.

CHAPTER NINE
THE GREY WOLF
(Making New Friends)

I had come to Tallahassee without a job and knowing absolutely nobody. The first week, I'd gotten up to go to the bathroom in the middle of the night, and feeling totally disoriented in the dark, fell down and gave myself a black eye. This meant I didn't have any kind of social life for two weeks, because I did not want to create a bad first impression with my bruised face making me look as though I'd been in a brawl. Finally, I felt ready to go out and conquer the world – or at least to make a few new friends – but how to go about it? In my mind, I transported myself to sit under my big oak tree in the woods, and soon I found myself staring into the wise eyes of a silver-haired she-wolf.

* * *

I jump up, startled, and prepare to run, but the wolf seems to be smiling.

"Nothing to worry about," the wolf says gently. "I'm not Big and Bad, and you're not Little Red Riding Hood."

"But you do have big teeth," I observe.

"The better to catch small creatures with, for our nourishment. Humans are not part of our diet."

"Then where did all the stories about wolves gobbling up little girls originate?"

"I have no idea," she says. "Probably in Mr. Grimm's imagination."

"Are you sure you're not lying to me, so you can put me at ease and then pounce —?"

"Research has shown that there has never been a documented attack by a wolf on a human being in North America – except for wolves with rabies – and I assure you I am a lot less rabid than some of your politicians. Relax yourself. I have much more to fear from you than you do from me. Now, permit me to advise you about making friends."

"What do you know about making friends?" I challenge the clever canine. "Aren't you supposed to be a loner?"

"*Au contraire,*" says the wolf, who I figure must have migrated from Canada. "Only the lowest fellows on the totem pole set out on their own, and since they can't catch much except mice and voles by themselves, they usually wind up joining another pack."

"That's right," I remind myself. "You are pack animals."

"*Mais oui,*" asserts the wolf. "Very much so."

"About how many in a pack?"

"It varies," the wolf says. "It can be three or four up to twenty or twenty-five. Around here a dozen is usual. It depends, you see, on how large the animals we wish to feed on. Once on a time, we used to dine on buffalo – until you avaricious humans began wiping out the herd."

"Not me," I defend myself. "I had nothing to do with it. That was way before my time."

The wolf continues to gaze at me with aloof indifference.

"So, how do you get into a pack?" I ask, glad to get the conversation off the sticky subject of American history.

"It begins with the family," the wolf says.

I inform her that my family is either dead or scattered, or both.

"*Quel dommage!*" she commiserates. "Then you must form yourself an artificial family."

"But how?" I ask.

"It is pronounced 'howl,' " she corrects me.

"What?"

"What you must do to gather the other wolves – pardon, I mean persons – to become part of your circle." She requests me to "witness," and throwing back her head she lets forth with a long, plaintive train whistle of a howl.

"Very nice," I compliment her.

"It's better when we do it in chorus," she informs me. "We like to take different notes and harmonize."

"I had no idea you were so musical," I admit.

"That's just part of it," she says. "It not only sounds more interesting than monotone, but it gives the impression that there are more of us than there actually are."

"But humans don't howl," I frown. "Except in pain."

The wolf looks up at me in amused tolerance. "What a dreadfully literal mind you have," she declares. "I am speaking of the poetic howl, the metaphorical howl."

"Oh." I stop and look again into her eyes. "I suppose you're trying to tell me that I must make my presence known. Somehow."

"I am not *trying* to tell you," the she-wolf says. "I am *telling* you; you are trying to understand."

"Yes, yes!" I say, with a mixture of enthusiasm and impatience. "I could write an article for the newspaper, get my name in print, perhaps act in community theatre – "

"It's possible," says the wolf. "Whatever is necessary to become visible. And audible. You are fortunate to have the telephone. Do not hesitate to use it."

I remember the days when I used to be terrified to make phonecalls, and how hard I worked to get over that phobia.

"And now, you will permit me, I have another suggestion," says the wolf.

"Yes?"

"It is more easy to meet many persons at the same time than attempt to meet individuals one by one. This is why we have developed, how you say, the conference call."

"Easier to meet people in groups," I repeat.

"Undoubtedly. When you consider how many of them are in your cities."

"So I should get myself into organizations of one kind or another."

"*Exactement*."

"Like the church or temple, or professional associations, or civic meetings – I should become a joiner."

"You make it sound like hard work," the wolf smiles. "Do you not know how to play?"

"Play what?" I ask.

"Just play," the wolf says. At this point we are joined by a raven, who hops around on the wolf's back. The wolf chases the raven. Then the raven chases the wolf. Another raven comes along and they play a game of "Sallujee" with a chestnut. The ravens then toss the chestnut into a puddle, laugh, and fly away.

"What was that all about?" I ask.

"Nothing at all," the wolf shrugs. "Just having fun."

"You guys know each other?"

"Oh, we're old friends," the wolf says.

"Speak for yourself!" cackles the raven, who has come back to perch on the wolf's head. "I'm not as old as all that!"

"You know what I mean," the wolf says. She explains to me that the raven tells the wolves where the caribou are hiding.

"And then they share the kill with us," the first raven says.

"When times get hard," the other raven says, circling overhead, "We eat the bugs that are in their fur."

"Hey that's what friends are fur!" says Raven Number One. They crack up laughing and zoom away again.

"But why a raven?" I whisper, in case the unpredictable black birds should unexpectedly appear again. "What do you have in common?"

"It is the most intelligent bird in the forest," the wolf explains. "Life is too short to bother with stupid ones."

I resolve to seek out the most intelligent people in my new surroundings, then decide to trust the wolf with my special problem. I'm experiencing a culture gap between the quick, aggressive northeast speech and the syrupy, conciliatory speech of the South. I'm afraid the people here won't like me because I'm a Yankee.

"Interesting," the wolf says. "One can misinterpret a friendly bite. Or the way another moves his tail. Excuse me, but let us continue our conversation a little over this way. There is a rattlesnake nearby."

"I don't hear anything," I say.

"Of course you do not," the wolf says. "My hearing is almost twice as good as yours. Nevertheless, I suggest you open your ears more frequently, and perhaps your hearing she will improve." She picks up her ears, till they are two pointy towers.

"At first listen more than you speak," she advises. "So that you may accustom yourself to the habits of the local people. And whatever you do, never tell people that they do things better where you come from. It will hurt their feelings."

"I had no ideas wolves were so considerate," I note.

"Does that surprise you? We never abuse our children, and we take care of our old and our sick. Do you?" Before I can come up with some kind of spin, she continues: "European fairy tales often depict me as a killer of men and the scourge of the village, but I assure you that my true nature is that of a nurturer. Are you not familiar with the story of Romulus and Remus?"

"The twins who founded the city of Rome?" I respond. "Yes, they were supposedly abandoned in the woods by their mother, a vestal virgin, ironically enough, but were nursed and raised by a she-wolf, until they reached manhood."

"That's just one of many legends about our warm and loving nature. Tu Kueh, the founder of Turkey, was reportedly suckled by a wolf, and so was Zoroaster. We are featured in the mythology of Germany, Ireland, the Aztec and Navajo – as wetnurses to great heroes."

"But those are just legends," I say.

"And so are the tales about the Wolf at the Door. You may choose to believe the positive or the negative. Which may provide a lesson to you. Always think the best about your fellow creatures, until you have reason to think otherwise."

"Getting back to the subject of making friends – " I put in.

"We never left the subject," the wolf corrects me. "It is not only the abandoned babies who need nurturing. All the world does. If you devote yourself to helping others grow, you will never lack for companions."

"Thank you," I say, daring to reach out and pet the wolf's soft fur. "You have been very helpful."

"You're welcome," the wolf says. "I am happy to aid you. And what will you do for me?"

"What do you want me to do?" I ask.

"Take my picture," says the wolf.

"But I didn't bring my camera," I apologize.

She stares at my chest, I look down and see that I have around my neck a brand new Polaroid.

"Where did this come from?" I mumble to myself.

"Where all dreams and wishes, prayers and meditations come from," answers the wolf. She goes up to a rock and poses, while I bring her into focus.

"You're wonderfully photogenic," I compliment her.

"I know," she grins. "Wait," she urges. She calls her husband, with short little whiny barks. He appears from the other side of the rock, tail straight out, staring at me with suspicion.

"Don't worry," she tells her mate. "They're not here to scalp us for our fur. I just want this person to take our picture, so we can show it to the kids." The couple nuzzle each other affectionately and I snap a couple of pictures of them. The he-wolf examines the finished photos.

"You've got me with my eyes closed," he complains. He's a lot grumpier than his wife.

"You always do that when I lick your nose," she giggles.

"And this one shows my scar."

"You should be proud of that scar," his wife cajoles him. "You struggled with a moose, and you won." He hugs her and grins a magnificent grin.

The she-wolf then drops her pose and comes over to me.

"Now let me take one of you," she offers.

"Do you know how?" I gasp in astonishment.

"It's just one of those point and shoot contraptions," she says. "I've watched humans open doors and work pulleys, and I've imitated those procedures. This is a piece of cake." She snaps my picture.

"Thanks," I say. "For everything."

"Not at all," says the she-wolf, politely. "We must depart now. It is time for choir practice."

"It was a pleasure to make your acquaintance," I say.

The wolves trot off aways, and then the she-wolf turns and faces me.

"I do not think you will have any trouble making new friends," she murmurs sweetly. "You and I already have an agreeable rapport. I appreciate especially that you are not judgmental. Feel free to call on us again."

CHAPTER TEN
THE EAGLE
(Acceptance versus Individuality)

Moving to a new city gives someone the opportunity to become a whole new person. But that only works if you know what kind of person you want to become, and what old habits, old ways of behaving you want to leave behind.

Coming to a slow-moving Southern city from a fast-paced Northern metropolis automatically demanded certain changes. I got rid of my navy blue, dark brown and grey wool suits, and bought bright-colored dresses and florals. I slowed down my speech in order to be understood, learned to say, "Hey," instead of "Hi," and perfected a couple of recipes to be used in the continual round of potluck dinners and "re-cip-tions." But the biggest change was in my relations with people. Survival in New York demanded a confrontational approach, including defensiveness, one-upsmanship and sarcasm. Here, I knew as soon as I bought my car that the old attitude wouldn't work. The new attitude seemed to be, "We can work it out," and "We can disagree without being disagreeable."

At first, I tried so hard to fit in, I actually dyed my hair blonde, because there seemed to be more blondes down here. But then I ran into the question – how much do I want to change myself in order to be accepted? Lizards protect themselves by protective coloration. They camouflage themselves to fit in with their surroundings. That's all very well if one wants to be a small, slimy reptile, slinking along close to the ground. I was faced with a dilemma: How can I be accepted in my new home, and still retain my individuality?

Every day I faced new challenges, met new people in new situations. Which "me" shall I present to them? I wondered. I was unsure and uncertain. My old methods no longer worked for me. To make matters worse, I developed a medical problem; I was plagued with sharp, stabbing pains in my stomach. When I went to the doctor for tests, she found nothing physically wrong with me. She ruled out stomach cancer, ulcers, gallstones, allergies. Finally, I was able to diagnose the problem myself. I have something I brought with me from my former habitat – an invisible worm eating at my insides – a worm called Fear.

* * * * *

"Do you play tennis?" the eagle asks me. He is sitting high atop a craggy tree. I am in my meditation mode, sitting amid rocks at the edge of a beach, with the woods behind me.

"I used to," I answer. "I used to be quite good, but I haven't played in awhile."

"Why don't we go down to the beach and bat some balls around?" the eagle invites me. I can think of half a dozen reasons why not to, but I don't want to hurt the bird's feelings.

"There's no net, for one thing," I respond.

"Oh, we can take care of that," the eagle assures me. He summons a pair of gulls, who go and bring two long, pole-like sticks. I hammer them into the wet sand with a rock. Within no time, the two gulls unravel a net and wind it around the two poles. Then they perch atop the poles, admiring their handiwork.

"Wish we could stay and watch the game," one of the gulls says, "but we only go to games where they serve popcorn." And the two of them fly away laughing.

"Are you ready?" the eagle asks me.

"I didn't bring my racket," I tell the eagle.

"I think I have an extra one, back at the eyrie," the eagle says. "I'll be right back." He flies up to the top of the tree again. While he's gone, I regret having consented to play with him, since I've never progressed beyond Advanced Beginner, and I'm afraid of looking ridiculous. I wonder why an eagle has been sent to me to teach me about Friendship and Fitting In, since this powerful predator is a very solitary type. For a moment I consider fleeing the scene, but realize I have nowhere to hide that this sharp-eyed aviator won't find me.

"Tennis is a test of character," I hear the eagle pronounce. He has swooped down behind me and is offering me a racket.

"How do you figure that?" I ask.

"You'll see," the eagle says. "Why don't I just lob some balls over the net, and you get some practice shots in. I'll serve you a few forehand and a few backhand."

The eagle tosses a few easy balls to my forehand, but then throws one short and I have to run in to volley.

"Ho, ho!" the eagle cackles. "Can't always expect things to come to you! Sometimes you've got to go after them!" I start getting a little nervous and miss the next ball. The one after that, I hit with the frame of my racket. "Relax!" the eagle calls. "I'm not going to send you any tricky ones. I'm going to do what any friend does for another friend – I'm going to bring out the best in you!"

I make a mental note of that aphorism, but when I swing at the next ball, which is towards my backhand, I barely get it over the net. "Can't seem to get up much power," I say.

"Power and speed come from being at the right place at the right time," the eagle encourages me. "Just think about connecting, that's all."

I think about it. I think about all the tennis lessons I'd ever had – the instruction to get the racket back, to watch my footwork, to keep my eye on the ball. The eagle is really good at that last part – his famous eyesight comes in handy as he catches every ball I send him with either his beak or his claw. Sets of instructions keep running through my brain. The eagle observes my tense posture and stops a moment.

"Just be natural," the eagle coaches me. "Do what feels comfortable." I swing the racket around in a few easy arcs, and soon my shots get better and better. I start feeling the right form happening throughout my body, instead of being a pattern in my mind.

"Let's rest a moment," I suggest.

"As you wish," the eagle says I sit down on a flat rock, and he perches on a rock above mine.

"Aren't you going to tell me what I've been doing wrong?" I ask.

"No," the eagle says. "You are quite well aware of what you have been doing wrong."

"I'm too lazy and lethargic to move when I have to move," I catalog. "And I tense up whenever anything comes at me." I listen to what I've just said. "Is that what you mean by Tennis being a test of Character?"

"Could be," says the eagle.

"I seem to be more focused on Competition than I am on Connecting, more concerned about Losing, than about Loosening Up," I laugh at myself.

"Old habits die hard," the eagle says. "Look at you. You're all out of breath and sweaty, and we weren't even keeping score. Let's go get some liquid refreshment." He then shows me a little waterfall, and we both take a drink of the cool, clear water. "Would you like to play a game?" the eagle asks.

"Not today," I say. "I want to talk to you about Fear."

"What are you afraid of?" the eagle asks.

"Everything," I answer. I tell him about the pains in my stomach. He just sits there, looking regal, the white mantle of feathers around his neck like a reward Nature has given him, a sign of respect. "I want to know," I continue, "Why it is that throughout the ages, and across many cultures, you have become a symbol of royalty and power."

The eagle adjusts his feathers and stares into space. I assume for a moment he has not heard the question. But there is nothing the matter with his hearing. He is considering his response.

"I dare to fly high," he says at last.

"Yes?"

"I dare to go after what I want."

"Yes, yes?"

"I dare to travel alone."

"Yes!"

"I dare to see what others cannot see or do not wish to see."

"You dare,' I repeat.

"I dare to dare," the eagle says.

"Does that mean you have no fear?"

"No," the eagle says. "It is only a fool who has no fear at all. But a hero or heroine, an artist or an activist finds ways to move through the fear."

"Right now," I confide in him, "I am in new surroundings, with the prospect of making new friends and new contacts."

"You are afraid of making the wrong move."

"Yes," I concur. "I'm afraid of missing my opportunities."

"The ball is coming at you," the eagle says.

"Right," I say, "And perhaps I am afraid of change, afraid of newness."

"Interesting," the eagle says. "And are there no others who can help you?"

"I need to seek them out," I say. "I want to meet people who are good for me, who are supportive and helpful and – well, like partners. "

"Birds of a feather," the eagle completes my thought. He's quick-thinking. I like creatures like that.

"Kindred souls," I elucidate.

"You want to meet people who are like you," the eagle says, staring at me with his hypnotic eyes. "And what are you like?"

"Well, I'm intelligent and energetic and – "

"Don't give me any superficial answer," the eagle says. "Don't swing at the ball before it's in the right place. I'm telling you that you won't be able to find people to help and love and support you unless and until you know who and what you are."

"Know thyself, as the Greeks said," I quote.

"Precisely," the eagle nods. "And not only must you know yourself; you must express yourself. Let people know how you feel about things."

"They might take offense," I say. "They might think I'm weird."

"Then they're not the right sort of folks for you."

"What you are telling me is that I must dare – to be myself."

"And it is only in Action that you will find yourself," the eagle adds. He rises into the sky. I admire his colossal wing spread, and hope that one day I, too, will be able to spread my wings the way he does, and fly high.

* * * * *

In a matter of weeks, I found that through pursuing my interests – Writing, Art, Politics – I attracted to myself a group of artists, writers and activists – older women, like myself, who have dared to be different. I call this happy group my "circle of krones."

CHAPTER ELEVEN
THE CORAL SNAKE
(Acquiring Wisdom)

Being a krone involves certain responsibilities. A krone, in folklore, is a wise woman, a good witch. That means she is supposed to have a great amount of wisdom. And she uses that wisdom to help others. When I lived in New York I was too busy working for a living and trying to survive to have the acquisition of wisdom as my goal. But now that I have more time, I'm not even sure how to go about becoming the wise woman I want to be.

In my meditation, I go back to a clearing in the woods. It is autumn, and heaps of colorful dry leaves are on the ground. They're not as colorful as the red maples and yellow oaks of New York State and New England, but North Florida does get a change of seasons, and there are orange-y brown leaves on the ground. I hear a rustling sound, and out of one of the piles of leaves emerges a snake, brightly banded in yellow, black and coral.

"You don't exactly believe in protective coloration, do you?" I begin.

"No, on the contrary," the snake replies, "What I have is called 'startle coloration.' It's supposed to scare my enemies into running away. It is so effective that the Kingsnake copies my coloration and it scares away his enemies, too."

"I hope I am not your enemy," I say.

"Not at all," the snake says. He wraps himself into a coil, but lifts his head to speak with me. "Only in Christian theology is the serpent reviled as the Evil One. Other cultures worship us. The aborigines of Australia associate us with the creation of life. In India, the cobra is considered the reincarnation of an important chief, and is depended on to bring wellbeing to the village. In other parts of Asia, serpents are regarded as fertility symbols. And in Central America we are considered the messengers to the rain gods."

"I notice that serpents adorn the caduceus," I add, "The symbol of the medical profession."

"Yes," the snake boasts. "That's because the Greeks regarded us as a symbol of reincarnation and healing. However, I am sent to you today because I also represent Wisdom."

"How did you get to represent Wisdom?" I ask. "You evidently don't have a very large brain."

"You're right about that," the snake admits. "I would have chosen the porpoise or the whale. But perhaps it has something to do with the shedding of my skin."

"I don't see how those two things have anything to do with each other," I declare.

"Don't you? In order to grow, I find it necessary to discard the old so that I may live in the new. Wisdom, I believe, has something to do with being willing to throw away old ideas and entertain new ones. It has to do with not being afraid of change and of challenge. At least," the serpent drawls, looking at me from under her sleepy eyelids, "that's what I've been told."

"I think I am willing," I tell the snake.

"Then you are already on the road to Wisdom," the snake informs me.

"How may I proceed further on the road?" I ask.

"Foolish people are very fussy about where Wisdom comes from," the snake drawls. "They look down on some sources as being unworthy to listen to. They decide that only certain books are valuable and others should be banned. They put labels on people, they invent 'isms.' Wise people know differently."

"What do they know?" I urge.

"They know that the Truth may come from anywhere at any time," the snake tells me. "That is why it is very important to stay alert, to listen to the voice of God in everyone and everything."

"Is there one great Truth, or are there many little truths?" I ask.

"Both," says the snake.

"Then I will seek them both," I say.

"Are you quite sure you want to do that?" the snake interrogates.

"Why, yes. Why shouldn't I?"

"Are you prepared to be cursed, reviled and despised, the way I am?" the snake asks.

"Well, I don't know," I frown. "Isn't it because of your venom that you are cursed, reviled and despised?"

"No," says the coral snake. "For I seldom use venom, except when attacked. It is because I speak truth to power."

"I see."

"No you don't. Not yet," the snake admonishes.

"But why don't people – ?"

"The lamp of truth exposes evil as well as good," the snake reminds me. "And a great many people are afraid to have that light shine on them."

"You asked me if I were prepared to be hated," I say. "How does anyone prepare for that?"

"You must love The Truth more than anything else in the world. More than your family, more than a lover. You must be willing to die for it. Many people have."

"Oh, dear," I sigh. "I'm not sure I'm willing to go that far."

"Look at the bright side," the snake suggests. "On your journey you will meet other truth-seekers, and they will be the most remarkable companions a person could have."

"How will I recognize them?" I inquire.

"You just will," the snake replies. "A yogi in one glance can recognize another yogi. But are you sure you wish it?"

"What choice do I have?" I ask. There are wrinkles on my face and flab has begun to creep into my arms and legs. My body is beginning to decay. Only in Wisdom can I still have power and enjoyment."

"That is true," the snake agrees. "Wisdom is the crown of the elderly. Now, shall I tell you a story?"

"Oh, yes!" I cry, clapping my hands like a little girl. "I love stories!"

"No doubt you have heard the legends about how Hercules killed snakes while he was in his cradle, and how St. Patrick drove the snakes out of Ireland. But let me tell you an Iroquois tale from the snake's point of view."

"That would be interesting," I encourage him.

"There was once a chieftain named Djisdaah, who was a great hunter, but he was cruel to animals. He derived special pleasure from killing and torturing snakes. One day another man from his village was walking through the forest and he heard a rustling sound. He crept closer to where the hissing came from and there in a great clearing was a great group of snakes, holding a war council.

"'For the sake of our children, we must not let this killing continue!' one of the snake leaders declared. "Let us go to their village and fight them!' And all the council members voted yes.

"The man crept away and ran back to the village to tell the people that the snakes were preparing to attack. Djisdaah knew that snakes were afraid of fire. He had personally burned a few himself. So he ordered the people of the village to drive wooden stakes into the ground all around the village, and when the snakes approached, he ordered the stakes to be set afire.

"But these snakes were determined to get their revenge, and they crawled right through the flames. Many of them died, but the brave ones continued, singing their war songs. Soon they reached the interior of the village, went into Djisdaah's hut and strangled him. Djisdaah's son then spoke to the snakes and said, 'Hear me, my brothers. You have won the battle. We surrender to you. What are your terms?'

"Then the earth trembled and cracked and a great snake, as tall as a pine tree, lifted himself out of the ground.

"'Hear me,' the great snake said. "I am the chief of all the snakes. We will go and leave you in peace but you must agree to two things.'"

"Djisdaah's son nodded his head. 'We will agree, Great Chief,' he said.

"'It is well,' said the Chief of the Snakes. 'These are the two things. First, you must leave my people alone and if you do, we will not bother you. Second, you must agree never to deem one of your men wise unless his Wisdom is accompanied by Respect for all living creatures.' And so it was agreed, and this became the law of the natural world."

I applaud heartily.

"Why are you clapping your hands?" the snake asks, and I realize he is unable to do that and doesn't understand that it means approval.

"I am showing you that I like your story," I tell him.

"The way to show me is to prove you have learned its lesson. There are those whom you humans deem wise. They are great warriors. They are teachers and medicine men. But they lack the traits of compassion and empathy, and therefore they are not wise at all."

"I will remember that," I say.

"Good," says the snake. "And if your wisdom is truly great, it will outlast you. It will make you immortal."

And with that, the snake unravels its coil and slithers silently away.

CHAPTER TWELVE
THE GREAT BLUE HERON
(Making Choices, Gaining Focus)

For the first time in my life I actually feel popular! A wallflower in high school (I didn't go to my senior prom!) and a shy, quiet girl in college (I started when I was sixteen, and always felt slightly out of it) I had only one close friend, who still is my best friend to this day. And now, I have my "circle of krones," all wanting me to accompany them to various activities around town. The downside of this spurt of popularity is that I am starting to feel scattered. There seem to be innumerable choices of things to do, and I feel torn in many directions.

"How can I maintain my sense of focus?" I ask. In my meditation, I am sitting on a sandy dune at the edge of a marsh. I see many wild birds – anhinga, grebe, quail – but they fly away. The one who remains is a great blue heron, standing profile, one leg raised, shoulders hunched, eyeing the water.

"What do you wish to focus on?" the heron asks me. He does not remove his eyes from the water. I start to tell him about projects I am working on, but still he does not turn his head.

"Would you mind looking at me when I'm talking to you?" I rebuke him.

"Yes, I would mind," the heron says. "You see, I am focusing on finding a fish."

"How long are you going to remain in that position?" I demand.

"As long as it takes," croaks the heron.

I have learned Lesson Number One. Impatience, perhaps my greatest fault, keeps me hopping from one task to another. I have lacked Perserverance, and that lack has been a stumbling block for me my whole life. I didn't wait for Love, before getting married, but jumped into a loveless relationship which was more like a business deal than a true partnership. I gave up, after a few rejections, on certain writing projects, only to see someone else come out with the book or play that I had envisioned.

"As long as it takes?" I repeat. "But what if it takes too long?"

"Sometimes," the heron says, "I stand here for hours. My hours are like your years. But if something is worth waiting for, then Waiting is the thing to do."

"That requires a certain amount of – " I begin.

"Confidence?" the heron asks.

"Yes, that," I say. "Confidence that eventually things will work out."

"Confidence that you and your work are deserving of acceptance?"

I nod. Lesson Number Two.

"I asked you before, about your focus," the heron says. "Let me put it another way. What are you committed to?"

"Writing," I answer easily.

"And what is your writing committed to?"

This gives me pause. I had never thought about that.

"Do you write just to make money?"

This makes me laugh. I know of no freelance writers who actually make a living at their writing, except for one, a journalist in Tampa, but his "living" amounts to under $20,000 a year. "If I wanted just to make money," I reply, "I would churn out romance novels or pornography, or silly articles for *Cosmopolitan* magazine."

"Money is no object?" the heron asks.

"Well, it is an object," I admit, "But not the only one. I care about subject matter. It's important to me that what I write is important."

"And what is important to you?"

"I have certain political views," I tell the waterfowl. "Unconventional ones. I want to share them."

"Go on," the heron urges.

"Views about peace," I explain, "and unity of all peoples. Views about tyranny and resistance to censorship and oppression."

"Good," says the heron. "Now we are getting somewhere."

"I am committed, also, to justice," I continue.

"Excellent," the heron says. "And how do you know what is right and what is wrong?"

"I try to get my guidance from God."

"Really?" the heron says. He turns his head at that, but immediately turns back again to his observation of the water. "And how do you do that?"

"I ask myself what it is that God wants me to do."

"If that is the case," the heron says, "I do not see that you have a problem. Except, perhaps, that you do not ask that question often enough."

Lesson Number Three. I am able to commit myself to short-range goals. Getting my car repaired, changing my prescription for eyeglasses, planning a meeting. It's the hidden goals, the long-range goals, where I run into trouble with Commitment.

"The answers do not always come clearly," I tell the heron.

"The still, small voice," the heron quotes.

"Beg pardon?"

"God spoke to his beloved leaders in a still, small voice," the heron says. "You must watch and listen for signs."

The concept of signs is new to me. I ask the heron for an example.

"How do I know there is a fish in the vicinity?" the heron queries me. "The water moves. It changes color. I feel a trembling, I hear a sound."

"I don't mean to seem disrespectful," I tell the heron, "But you have just one talent. You are gifted at catching fish. My problem – and it really is a problem – is that I have many talents. And in trying to find outlets for them all, I tend to spread myself too thin."

"Your talents are merely the claws, the talons, the beak, the eyes. Your talents are the means to an end. Never take your eyes off your main purpose."

"And now," I tell the heron, "I have many friends. And in spending time with all of them, I also feel my time is being frittered away."

"Your friends are only friends if they help you achieve your main purpose."

"That goes for men, too, I suppose?"

"It certainly does," the heron replies. "We are not bothered by that thing you humans call Romance." I hang my head shamefacedly, thinking of the many hours, days, weeks I wasted answering and placing personals ads and going on one or two dates with men in the hopes of finding True Love. "When you are on the right path," the heron adds, "the right companions will accompany you."

How simple he makes it sound, I think to myself. And yet, simplicity is what I am seeking. I want to simplify my entire life, and the steadfast heron is showing me the way. "Thank you!" I cry, overcome with gratitude. I am about to walk away.

"Wait," the heron says. "Your impatience is showing again."

"Sorry," I apologize. "I thought you were finished speaking."

"You really must learn to slow down," the heron admonishes. "If you want to thread a needle, you cannot possibly succeed if you keep on moving the eye." I come back and sit down, cross-legged, in a yoga position of relaxation.

"That's better," says the heron. "If you are constantly in a posture of defense, you will keep out the good along with the bad."

"I'm listening," I tell my fine feathered friend. And this time I mean it.

"I want to give you an exercise," the heron says.

"An exercise?"

"Finish this sentence," the heron orders me. He does look authoritative, with his crown of beautiful feathers. "I am."

"I am what?"

"Yes. What are you? Tell me five things."

"I am a writer," I begin. "A mother, a friend, an actress, a teacher – "

"Now tell me one thing that sums up all the rest."

I close my eyes and breathe deeply, sitting in the silence. I don't know where the words come from. Perhaps from the still, small voice:

"I am – an educator," I say slowly.

"Ah," says the heron. "Now, don't forget it. Be nothing else, do nothing else, but that great thing you are."

The heron suddenly ducks his head and long, snake-like neck under the water and comes up with a struggling mullet.

CHAPTER THIRTEEN
THE MALLARD
(Being a Teacher)

Inspired by the goal of becoming a real educator, I took a job as an adjunct English instructor at the community college. I taught Freshman English and also the second-year course, which was called "Writing Argument and Persuasion." I was really looking forward to the "Argument" course, since it involved inculcating the basic principles of Logic, and, or so I thought, would also provide an opportunity for lively discussion of ideas.

I had not taught this particular age group for some time. My last teaching posts in New York City involved teaching writing courses or English as a Second Language to adults who were highly motivated to learn. But an entire generation had gone by, and I encountered a very different breed of student either from the kind that I had been myself, or the kind I remembered from twenty years ago. What I ran into now were students who did not want to discuss ideas. They didn't want to improve their written English. They basically wanted to do as little work as possible, get handed an Associate degree, and go out and get a high-paying job. I was dealing with the manipulative, passive-aggressive "Generation X."

From the very beginning of the semester, most of the students tried to con me – pretending numerous funerals – of grandmothers, grandfathers and favorite aunts – as an excuse for taking off for the weekend to attend an out-of-town football game. They purloined written work off the Internet or borrowed it from friends and tried to pass it off as their own. Absenteeism was rampant, so I never was teaching the same group of students twice and was therefore unable to follow up on material I'd already taught.

I'd started college when I was sixteen and was awestruck at the number of books in the library; I wanted to read every one! These students hated to read. Most of them were never even in the habit of reading a newspaper. Any reading assignment over three pages long was regarded by them as a gross imposition on their valuable time – time they preferred to spend going to bars and having parties. Out of each roster of twenty-five students, I had maybe three I could actually call "students." The others I called "enrollees" or "registrants."

I was frustrated, I was angry, and I was bored seeing the students make the same dumb grammatical mistakes again and again. I wished I could up and quit, but I needed the money. I felt I needed a vacation, long before Christmas rolled around. So I took one, in my mind.

* * * * *

I go, in my meditation, to the edge of a small lake, or perhaps it can better be called a large pond. There, a mother duck is waddling along the bank, a train of baby ducks following close behind.

"Ah, a fellow teacher!" I exclaim. "Why don't I ask her?"

"Ask her what, what, what?" the duck quacks at me.

"How do you become an inspiring teacher?" I ask. "And what do you do if the youngsters don't want to learn?"

The mallard, for that's the kind of duck she is, instructs her brood to sit down and wait for her and not to venture into the water without her. Then she waddles over to me.

"First," she says, "You must instill discipline and order. Order, order, order! You can teach nothing without that, that!" I compliment her on how well she literally keeps her ducks in a row.

"But what do you do if they get out of line?" I want to know.

"I peck at 'em until they shape up," she replies quickly. "Whack! Whack!"

"What would you say is your most successful teaching method?" I inquire.

"I teach primarily by example," she proclaims. "Every good teacher does. I show them how to swim, and then I tell them to copy me, till they've got the knack, knack!"

"You mean give them samples of my own writing?"

"No, I mean be the kind of person they admire. Show them how happy and contented you are. Then they'll say to themselves, 'I want some of that, that!'"

What this master teacher has to tell me is so interesting to me, I soon find myself overlooking her speech defect, which evidently involves an obsessive compulsive attempt to rhyme everything with "Quack."

"But," I argue, "so many of them admire nothing but wealth. They are aware of how little an adjunct instructor makes, and they don't want any of my poverty."

"They must see how important writing skills are in their daily lives," the duck frowns.

"The only writing they do is e-mail," I explain. "And no one seems to care how terrible that is."

"Do you show them samples of good writing?" the duck asks me.

"Of course," I reply. "I give them examples of good writing," I complain, "but they don't want to read them. They want to duplicate the same silly, formulaic compositions they wrote in high school and got "B" on. They want everything to be easy. And writing is hard."

"But perhaps your standards are too high? I can't turn my babies into peacocks or swans. Not every student takes the same tack. Not everyone can be crackerjack!"

"I thought of that," I say, considering the possibility again. "But there are certain requirements for the course, and they're not meeting the requirements. It's as if you told your kids it's time to migrate, and they said 'We don't feel like migrating.' How can I teach if they don't want to learn?"

"You can't," the duck answers. "They must take their share of responsibility. Teaching is a partnership, not a one-way track."

"Did you ever have a child who refused to learn how to swim?"

"Yes, I did," the duck recalls. "Slack, slack."

"What happened to him?"

"Her. It was a female. She drowned. Alas and alack."

I drew back, startled.

"It's that simple," the duck announces. "Swim or sink. I tell them that at the very outset, so we understand each other completely. 'Here are my rules,' I tell them. 'You wander off and make your own rules, you're going to get eaten alive, and nobody can save you.' That scares them a bit. Takes them aback, aback."

"I don't think mine are afraid of me," I muse. "Students used to be a little in awe of their teachers. They're not any more. I think maybe because they're not afraid of their parents. They push their parents around, and they think they can do the same with all adults."

"Give 'em a test," the duck suggests. "Let 'em see how they stack, stack."

"What?"

"That'll put the fear of God into 'em," she grins. "Give 'em a test. Let them see for themselves what they need to do to get on track."

"I don't want them to get completely discouraged," I say.

"Why not?" the duck inquires.

"Why, then, they might drop out of the class!"

"Would that be so terrible?" the duck counters. "Might teach the others a valuable lesson."

"Yes, indeed it might," I agree.

"Crack down about attendance," the duck commands. "Crack, crack!" I think she forgets I'm not one of her charges. "You're eider here or you're not here."

"Eider? Isn't that a kind of duck?"

"That was a wisecrack, a wisecrack!" the duck informs me. "You're not here three times, and you're out. Period."

"And the ones who are left?"

"Talk to them one at a time. Individual conferences. Most of them think they can get lost and hide in a pack, pack. Take each one aside and tell them what they need to do in order to meet your standards and in order to pass the course. And praise them. Tell them what they've done well. Tell them you have high hopes for them, but you won't take any flak, flak!"

"I've done that," I sigh. "They just don't seem to want to be in school at all."

"Where would they rather be?" the duck asks.

"On some other planet, I believe."

"Eating the wrong snack," the duck mutters. "Possibly on smack or crack."

"What's that you say?"

"Taking the wrong substances into their body," the duck suggests. "If they go and eat some poisonous plant, you can argue with them 'til you're blue in the face, but their brain is too messed up for them to process what you're saying. They really have left the planet, and it's a waste of your time to try to run after them and rescue them. Sometimes you just can't bring them back, back!"

"That's right, you said the right word," I tell this maternal figure. "I feel that I want to rescue them all. They're sad, they're depressed, they're alienated – "

"And you are going to make up for all the failures of their parents and the society?" the duck challenges me.

"I'd like to," I admit.

"I see the problem," the duck says. "Your ego is too heavily involved. It's weighing you down."

"My ego?" I echo.

"You and I are only receptacles in God's hands. We must pray to let God's ideas flow to our students through us."

"Do ducks pray?" I asked.

"I can't speak for other ducks," the mallard says, "but every day I pray to God to keep my little ones safe from attack, attack!"

"And is there a prayer for teachers?" I ask.

"I'll tell you the one I use," the duck responds. "Here it goes: 'Lord, make me your instrument,' I ask. 'I am here, Lord, willing to do what is necessary to express and reveal your goodness.'"

"I like that," I smile. For some reason, I feel a great sense of relief, and tell the duck so.

"Naturally," the duck says. "You can't carry the whole world on your back! That's God's job. If you try it," she advises, "you will accomplish nothing except to ruin your own health. Why put yourself on the rack, rack?"

I think for a minute. Shall I revise all my grades upwards, as so many other teachers do, to make the kids feel good?

"I like these kids!" I hear myself wailing. "In spite of their rotten attitude and their lack of background, they are sweet and vulnerable and good, and I want to help them! I don't want them to go out in the world unprepared!"

"Then concentrate on the ones who do want to learn," Professor Mallard advises. "Give them everything you've got. Let the others listen in, if they care to. If they don't care to, that's their problem, not yours. Let them get left back, back! You can't take up the slack, slack!"

"I always maintained that the principal of democratic public education, of equal opportunity enrollment, meant that everyone has a right to an education."

"Everyone has the right to enroll in school," the duck says. "They don't all have the right to graduate. Not unless they earn it." She cocks her head at me, and quacks, "That's a fact!" Then she excuses herself and patters over to her ducklings, who have tucked their heads under their wings and fallen asleep. "Watch this!" she winks at me. She sets up a tremendous cackle and flaps her wings about furiously till they make a whirring noise. The ducklings stand up, startled, shaking their feathers. "Sometimes they need a good wake-up call," the duck smiles at me. "Shock 'em outa the sack!" Then, lining up her offspring, she heads for the water, her little golden balls of fluff mimicking her every movement.

* * * * *

I followed the mother duck's advice, cracked down on attendance, gave numerous tests and handed out "D"s and "F"s on papers that deserved them, offering the opportunity to improve the grade with a rewrite. Within a few weeks, I had only five or six students left in each class. The administration said they didn't care; they'd gotten the money for the class and it was too late to make refunds. But I cared. This was not what I envisioned the life of an educator to be.

So I made a switch out of the classroom, into another type of teaching situation. I worked part time at the Writing Center of the college, helping individual students with their papers.

I enjoyed the one-on-one situation, the opportunity to get to know each student through his or her written work. I don't remember ever revealing to teachers such intimate details of my personal life. These papers dealt with alcoholism, drugs, rape, hatred of family. Evidently, today's students have very few adults in their life to turn to. I sometimes felt that their papers were cries for help. Frequently I wrote comments on them that gave the student something to think about. Often I would write in red ink, "Come and see me and let's discuss this."

But my compassionate comments began to get me in trouble. My supervisor told me that my job entailed only writing notes on the papers regarding organization and grammar. "ROS" for "Run on Sentence." "Org" for Organization. "Frag" for Fragment. But when one student wrote about waking up naked on a beach after a night of drinking, thinking she had probably been raped, and the "Conclusion" in her paper was "I will only drink with people I know," I wrote a comment questioning Drinking as an ongoing social activity, and asking if she'd ever heard of Date Rape. My supervisor called me into her office. I was given a warning.

CHAPTER FOURTEEN
THE BEAR
(Strength in Misfortune)

What's a person to do when everything goes wrong at once? Where do you find the strength to continue? Within a two-week period, I was let go from a part-time job I really liked, was in a minor fender-bender which was about to cost me a pretty penny in car repairs, and lost the keys to my house.

I was feeling particularly rotten about losing the job, since I believed it was due to a misunderstanding. I'd been working in the Writing Lab at the community college, enjoying the one-on-one interactions with the students, and feeling really useful in helping people improve their writing skills and prepare papers for their classes. I'd always prided myself in being strict, but fair. But two students misinterpreted things I said, and evidently the standards are different here from the other schools where I've worked. I was told my expectations of the students were too high. They can be admitted to the community college with a "D" average, and this would be all right, in my opinion, if they realized that they were below par and struggled to improve. But so many want to slide through unscathed by any semblance of learning, just to get their hands on an AA degree, in the belief it will guarantee them a high-paying job. I would have fought the discharge, but since I was an adjunct, I apparently had no rights.

The car accident was my fault. I was upset and in a fog about the job, and backed into a car in a parking lot. The keys? I lose my keys frequently. It's my way of telling myself I'm upset and asking me to figure out what the problem is and what to do about it.

"God give me strength!" I appealed in my woodsy retreat in the land of meditation. I looked up and saw a large brown bear, standing at attention.

* * *

"Here I am!" she bellows. I know it is a female bear, because she is wearing a large, flowered pocketbook over her shoulder.

"Are you trying to tell me that you are God?" I ask.

"No, of course not, silly. I am Strength."

"And what am I supposed to do with you?"

"I don't know," says the bear. "You're the one that asked for me."

"I do feel I need protection," I say, tears welling up in my eyes. "I'm feeling alone and unable to cope."

"Then borrow me," the bear says.

"Borrow you?"

"I will be your protector. I will fight your demons for you."

"I don't see how. I'm not about to schlep a bear around with me on job interviews and to car repair shops."

"The way it works is this," the bear says, assuming a more relaxed pose, as she waddles over to me. "The universe functions something like a bank, with everything you need in it. You can borrow anything you want from that bank at any time you choose, providing your credit is good. And yours obviously is."

"I've heard about bulls and bears in the stock market," I quip. "Didn't realize they were in banking as well."

"Right now," my benefactress tells me, "I think you need a hug." She embraces me, and for some reason I feel no fear. I inhale her scent, which is like all the spices and perfumes of the world, combined into a dizzying aroma. I feel that I am warmed by the symbol of Mother Russia, my ancestry, and that all my ancestors have combined in this ursine creature to remind me of my lineage and my legacy. Her affectionate, accepting gesture gives me permission to relax, and I find myself weeping profusely, until the fur on the bear's shoulder is wet with my tears.

"There, there," the mother bear says, "It'll be all right."

"You're so strong and powerful, you probably wouldn't understand what I'm going through right now," I tell the bear. "Everything is going wrong in my life – all at the same time! Has that ever happened to you?"

"It certainly has," the bear says. She leans her back up against a tree and twists herself back and forth, to scratch herself. "I remember one day I went fishing, and every single fish wriggled away from me! Not only that, I slipped on a wet rock and fell in the water, bumping my head!"

"What did you do?" I ask.

"I told myself, 'This is not a good day for fishing,' and I went in search of a beehive to get me some honey."

"There's a lesson in there somewhere, I suppose," I say with a frown.

"When everything goes wrong, the universe is trying to tell you something. It is taking you by the scruff of your neck and shouting to you: 'CHANGE DIRECTION!'"

"But I really loved that job!" I argue. "I felt I really belonged there!"

"But the people there didn't think so," the bear reminds me. "And if they didn't think so, then you didn't."

"My wallet was stolen, too," I pout.

"Where was that?"

"There, in the writing center. By one of the students. When I went to get her an exercise on sentence structure."

"That was just in case you didn't hear it the first time. It was an echo, saying 'CHANGE DIRECTION!'"

"'Change direction?' I reiterate. "I have no idea which direction to go in now. I have been a teacher all my life!"

"Perhaps it is time to consider other options," the bear suggests. "Perhaps, now that your fish have eluded you, there is a beehive waiting for you somewhere."

"But that's just one thing that's wrong," I protest. " I told you that everything – "

"Oh, yes. The car."

"Among other things."

"You were in the driver's seat."

"Yes, unfortunately, I was."

"You seem to think you are always in the driver's seat. You are unwilling to let God and God's representatives chart your course."

"Oh, great!" I mock her. "You want me to take my hands off the wheel?"

"Only figuratively," the bear says. "There is an American Indian poem which goes like this: 'Sometimes I stumble and fall and feel all of Fate is against me. Then I lift my feet off the ground and am carried by great winds across the sky.'"

"That's beautiful," I tell her. "Thank you. And what about the keys?"

"Keys represent knowledge. You feel you have insufficient knowledge to make the big decisions you need to make. On a more literal plane, perhaps the universe is telling you it is time to leave that house, being as the universe locked you out of it."

"I am feeling a bit oppressed by home ownership," I admit. "Mowing lawns, making repairs, or trying to find reliable repairmen to do so. Sometimes I feel I'd like to sell the house, live in a rented apartment, and use the money I make on the sale for travel."

"Well then, I guess we've solved your problems," the bear says. "Tomorrow you'll check the want-ads and go see a real estate agent."

"But wait, there's more!" I tell the she-bear, now that I've got her ear and she's proven to be such a good listener. "The other day, I cut my finger with a knife while chopping vegetables. And on top of everything, I got the flu."

"You are crying out for help," the bear says. "You are unable to do all that you have undertaken to do all by yourself. So why don't you confide in your friends? Perhaps they will help you see which direction you are meant to go in."

"I don't want to burden my friends with my problems," I tell her. "Besides, Tallahassee is like a small town in many ways. People gossip a lot."

"Then perhaps you need to go into hibernation for awhile."

"You mean live in a cave?"

"Not exactly. But since everything you do lately seems to turn out wrong, why not do nothing for awhile?"

"Yes!" I agree. "Why not! At least it would prevent more horrible things from happening! I keep thinking, Okay, God, what's the next plague you are gonna – "

"Pardon me for interrupting," the bear says, "but bears are not known for their manners. I want to ask you a question."

"Yeah, what!" I sigh.

"Where is your faith?"

"Faith! Ha! That's a good one! It's easy to have faith when things are going along smoothly, when your hopes are being fulfilled and you're getting your way. But when your whole life seems to be slipping into the sewer – "

"That's when you need faith the most," attests the bear. "That's when you need, if you'll pardon the pun, to bear witness."

"I never knew what that meant," I confess. "Bear witness."

"It means to live in the moment, and to collect evidence of God's existence."

"Collect evidence."

"You seem to be reenacting the Book of Job," the bear observes. "You'll recall that God was testing his faith, too. And do you recall what evidence he found that in spite of his misfortunes there was goodness in the universe?"

"I'm not much of a Bible reader," I confess.

"God appears to Job in a whirlwind, and recounts to him all the wonders that He can perform – from the creation of the universe, to the thunder and rain, to the power of the behemoth and leviathan. And do you remember what Job answers, when he is finally humbled?"

"I told you, I don't go around citing chapter and verse."

"He said, 'I uttered that I understood not; things too wonderful for me, which I knew not.' Y'see, Job realized that he had been unable to see the whole picture."

"The whole picture?" I ponder. "Like in the 'through a glass darkly' bit?"

"You see what is happening to you, but you do not see why it is happening," the bear elaborates. "When you see the why of a problem, you are able to grin and bear it."

"Ouch! Another clumsy pun," I comment.

"I'm a clumsy bear," the ursine critter reminds me. "Big animals, who think in big terms, are often clumsy. What of it?"

"And I suppose you do see the why of every problem?" I challenge her.

"No," the bear says, lowering her head, "for I am just a poor mortal creature like you. But I do know one thing."

"What's that?"

"That both the sources of all our problems – and the solutions – are within us."

"I knew that," I say.

"Then why are you sad?" the bear questions me. "If such an awkward creature as I can learn how to box and to dance, then surely you can achieve much more."

"You know how to box and to dance?" I ask, amazed.

"Oh, yes. I was taught by a gypsy showman. Put 'em up!" and she strikes a boxing pose. We spar for a few moments, and then she says, "Let's call it a draw. I prefer dancing!" She takes my two hands in her front paws, and does a little jig-like balance, then walks me around in a slow version of a square-dance swing. Finally, she lifts me up and sits me down on a tree stump.

"You are remarkable!" I laugh.

"Not so remarkable as you," the bear says. "I am here to remind you of the unlimited power of the human mind."

"Unlimited?"

"If I were the jealous sort, I would envy you! Your conscious mind is critical, analytical, judgmental, capable of absorbing and categorizing information. But then you also have a subconscious mind which is open, creative, intuitive! What wonders you can achieve with this inventive, infinitely fertile thing called the mind!"

"Well, I'm not doing myself much good with it these days," I complain, lapsing into my habitual kvetchiness.

"Oh, but you are!" the bear contradicts me.

"How do you figure that?"

"Your consciousness attracts to you the experiences your soul needs, in order to grow!"

"So getting fired was – "

"To teach you what your real work is!"

"And the accident – "

"To teach you to pay attention to the present moment!"

"And the keys – "

"To show you the way to the place where you will be most comfortable!"

"You see every mistake, every misadventure as a lesson?" I inquire.

"Every blessed one!" the bear grins.

Oh, great, I think to myself. I ask for Strength, and I'm given a Pollyanna. "If you don't mind my asking," I say, "What's in that bag you are carrying?"

"I thought you'd never ask!" she roars. "I was wondering, on my way over here, what I would say to you, and so I consulted this." She pulls a book out of her knapsack. Wouldn't you know, it's a Bible! "I just opened a page at random, the way I heard St. Augustine had done, and guess what I found?"

"Tell me."

"Revelations Twenty-one. Listen." She opens the book, where she has placed a flower as a bookmark, and reads to me: "'And I saw a new heaven and a new earth: for the first heaven and the first earth were passed away....And I saw the holy city, new Jerusalem, coming down from God out of heaven....and I heard a great voice out of heaven saying Behold, the tabernacle of God is within men and he will dwell with them....'"

"Coincidence," I say.

"Synchronicity," she corrects me. "I continue. 'And God shall wipe away all tears from their eyes; and there shall be no more death, neither sorrow, nor crying, neither shall there be any more pain: for the former things are passed way. And he that sat upon the throne said, 'Behold, I make all things new.'"

"Now, that's encouraging," I admit.

"Do you understand what it means?" the bear asks. "He makes all things new. Every day you have a new beginning. New skin, new blood, new ideas, new possibilities – "

"New possibilities – " I repeat.

"Wait," the bear says, "One more phrase. 'And he said unto me, It is done.' I think that means that what is over is over, and we shouldn't wallow around in the muck of the past. And here's the best part. God says, 'I am Alpha and Omega, the beginning and the end. I will give unto him that is athirst of the fountain of the water of life freely. They that overcometh shall inherit all things; and I will be their God, and they will be my children.'"

"Did Job overcome?" I ask.

"Oh, yes," the bear assures me. "He lived a hundred and forty years, and had seven sons and three daughters, beautiful children, all of them. I remember them well."

"You?"

"Oh, dear, I guess the secret is out. I'm an angel bear."

"You said you were mortal!"

"I lied. Not even angels are perfect."

"A new Jerusalem," I mused. "I like that."

"I thought you would," the bear says, putting the book back in her knapsack, and slinging it over her shoulder. "And you can be one of its builders. If."

"If I change direction?"

"And move your mind into the field of the All-Possible, knowing God is with you, in you and surrounding you with love."

As my angel bear waves goodbye to me, I realize that God is bigger than any problem that can occur in my life. I am ready to become an instrument of the Almighty.

CHAPTER FIFTEEN
THE PRAYING MANTIS
(Telling the Universe)

It was difficult, finding a part-time job in Tallahassee to replace the teaching job I had. The most difficult thing in jobhunting, I found, was to keep one's spirits up. In a society where the first thing people ask you when they meet you is, "What do you do?" or "Where do you work?" you tend to feel like an outsider when you don't have a job. And when other people measure you by your income, you tend to feel worthless when no income is coming in.

I never even told most of my friends that I was no longer teaching at the college. I silently read the want-ads over breakfast and applied for countless state jobs, where I couldn't even get an interview. I was tempted to take anything – proofreader at minimum wage; salesgirl with a six-day-a-week schedule; secretary, nanny – did I dare to ask for what I really wanted? I wasn't even sure what I wanted was out there. Maybe I was too old?

I was looking not only for a source of income, but something that would be interesting, creative and constructive, something that would also give me a "presence" in the community. I looked back over the many jobs I'd had and realized how few of them were emotionally and intellectually fulfilling. I get depressed when I think of past failures. Perhaps it was time to start thinking about making a contribution.

"Be ashamed to die," Horace Mann said, "Until you have done a good deed for Humanity." I knew that because it was on a statue in the middle of campus at Antioch College, my alma mater.

I wanted to pray about finding a new career path, but I'd never really prayed, and I wasn't sure I knew how. "Is there a right way to pray?" I wondered. "Who or what am I praying to?" and "Hello. Is anybody out there who hears prayers and answers them?"

* * *

I go to my sacred space, and wouldn't you know, a praying mantis hops down from a leaf in front of me, where he has been invisible until now. He stares at me with his bulging eyes, and demonstrates the prayer position.

"I see what the position is," I tell the gentle insect, pressing my hands together, "but I'm not sure what the purpose is."

"You know what meditation is, don't you?" the insect interrogates me.

"Of course," I reply. "I'm doing it right now."

"All right. In meditation you are receiving messages from the universe. Prayer simply reverses the process. You are sending messages to the universe."

"But is anybody listening?" I want to know.

"Maybe yes, maybe no," the mantis shrugs. "Pascal's wager. Fifty-fifty chance."

"Then why do it?"

"It may or may not influence the universe," the mantis tells me. "But it has a pretty good effect on you."

"What effect?"

"It clarifies what it is you want and need."

"I know what I want and need," I tell the insect. "A job. I want to know how I ask God to give me a job."

"Ha! Do you think God is running a personnel agency?" the mantis sniffs.

"No, but if He or She or It is all-powerful, maybe – "

"You want some magic words, maybe? Like hocus-pocus chiminy-ocus?"

"Well, maybe some words would get me a dull and low-paying job, and other words might get me an interesting, higher paying one."

"Looka here, kiddo," the mantis says to me, "Let me tell you what Prayer is not."

"I thought it could be anything we wanted it to be– "

"Wrong," says the mantis. "Prayer is not a shopping list. It's not about making specific demands, like 'Please God let me pass the finals' or 'Please God let me win the lottery.' Prayer is not about Control; it is about Consciousness."

"Consciousness of what?"

"Of the interconnectedness of all things." The insect calls my attention to a beautiful spider web, covered with sparkling droplets of dew. "The Hindu sages told of The Web of Indra," the mantis continues. "Indra, The God of All the Heavens, held the web of existence wherein every intersection has a knot, in every knot, a jewel. And in every jewel is a reflection of every other jewel."

"The web," I repeat, in my literal way. "I could search for a job on The Web."

"The Upanishads also speak of the Wheel of Creation," the mantis continues. "It contains all the elements, all the senses, all the desires, the ways of knowing, the ways of doing. If any part of it moves, the entire wheel moves."

"And what is at the center of the wheel?" I ask.

"The Spirit," the mantis says, "the Eternal."

"So, how do I get the wheel moving?" I demand.

"Seek to connect to the spirit," the mantis says. "And then let go of your attachment to results. Don't forget that you are not the center, you never were the center, you never will be the center."

"That sounds awfully vague to me," I complain. "Can't you direct me to a practical shortcut?"

"Practical? She wants practical.," the mantis shrugs. "Well, for starters, you might try reaching the Oversoul through the souls of others around you."

"I suppose we could call them 'spokes-persons,'" I quip, never able to resist a pun.

"Get wheel," the mantis throws back at me.

"One good turn deserves another," I return.

"Axle no questions, I'll tell you no lies," says the mantis without batting an eye. I realize that when it comes to pun wars, I am in the presence of a samurai. "Now, how many people have you told that you are seeking a new job?" he asks.

"None," I answer. "I've been so embarrassed about losing the last job."

"I see," says the mantis. "But if you don't express what your goals are, how do you expect to achieve them?"

"You keep pretty quiet about your prayers," I remind the mantis.

"Thoughts can be heard by the universe," the mantis tells me. "Powerful thoughts can influence outcomes."

"Do you believe that?" I ask the mantis, my skepticism showing.

"Why shouldn't I?" says the mantis, who loves to answer a question with a question. "And you will, too, if you really think about it. I'll bet you can think of at least three times when your thoughts influenced events."

"You seem to be a betting sort of creature," I observe.

"It's my biggest vice," the mantis tells me. "I sometimes jump without looking where I'm going. It's not a good idea. Better to pray beforehand."

"Three times where my thoughts–?" I repeat.

"Influenced outcomes."

"Why three?"

"In Kabbalah, it's a lucky number. Go ahead."

"Yes," I begin, "there was the time I told a friend that the sort of man I was looking for was tall and dark and gangly had a cleft chin like me. He would be in the arts and have curly hair. And then I walked into a poetry workshop in Greenwich Village, and there he was – the spitting image of my description – teaching the class. There was instant attraction on both sides. I had just forgotten to mention one thing. That he should be unattached."

"He was married?"

"No, but he was involved with a young woman half his age, and his ego would not permit him to break off that relationship."

"Be careful what you ask for," the mantis reminded me.

"Another time," I continue, "I wanted a clock radio for Christmas. My parents never gave me presents, and my son was still a student and couldn't afford such a gift. Two days before Christmas, I was walking along the street in New York City, and on top of a garbage pail, I see a clock radio. There's a note attached to the top of it. The note says, 'This radio works. All it needs is a light. Enjoy, enjoy! Merry Christmas!'"

"Sounds like a *mechiah* to me," the mantis says.

"A what?"

"Hebrew for 'miracle.' Got another one?'"

"Well, maybe the glove," I respond.

"The glove?"

"Yes. I found a black and tan Isotoner left-hand glove one day in New York City. And I said to myself, 'What good is only one glove?' I wished I might find a matching glove, but of course I thought I never would. The very next day, on the other side of town, I find a matching Isotoner right-hand glove."

"Wonderful!" the mantis applauds.

"And then there was the time I found a beautiful unframed engraving when I was on my way to Brighton Beach. And the next day I found a picture frame just the right size. And the time I wished for a thousand dollars so I could go on a trip, and the next day my tax refund comes and it's for nine hundred and ninety-nine dollars and fifty cents."

"Enough, enough," says the mantis. "You proved my point. What happened to the other fifty cents?"

"Maybe I didn't wish hard enough," I muse.

"Could be," the mantis agrees. "So you see, praying works."

"I guess," I have to admit.

"And I'm telling you it works even better if you verbalize your wishes. But only in a positive way."

"What do you mean?"

"What I mean is, how many thoughts do you think you can have in your head at the same time?"

"Only one, I guess," I answer.

"So, if you're thinking 'Don't let me get robbed," and you keep saying that to yourself again and again – guess what's gonna happen? You're gonna get robbed! If you're thinking "I don't want to go out with an alcoholic,' next thing you know, alcoholics will beat a path to your door. It's a basic law of the universe."

"So I should not think about the kind of job I don't want, just about the kind that I do want?"

"Exactly. And maybe you could also think what you're going to give to the universe to say thank you. That's called a covenant. They come in handy."

"I will!" I cry. "And do you think I should go ahead and tell people about the kind of job I'm looking for?" I ask.

"It wouldn't hurt," the mantis says. "But do so without expectations. Remember, you do the what; God does the how."

"I think I'm going to need another miracle," I mutter.

"Okay," the mantis says. "Watch this." The insect then demonstrates to me one of his remarkable powers. He rotates his head completely around on its axis. "I did that to teach you a lesson," he says.

"What lesson is that?"

"You never know what direction a miracle is coming from," he says. "So be on the lookout."

"Were you a yogi?" I ask the mantis. "In another life?"

"No" the mantis says. "I was a rabbi."

* * * * *

Following the advice of the bright green bug, I prayed not for a job but for guidance, not for money but for openness and receptivity. In addition, I told all my friends that I was looking for a part time job in the arts. Within a week, a friend of mine sent me an email telling me she'd noticed an ad for a website which is looking for an arts reviewer. A website! It was meant to be! I exclaim. The web of interconnectedness!

I emailed the Content Editor, and he asked for writing samples. I sent a few clips and in a few days the Content Editor called me in for an interview. I liked his openness, honesty and sense of humor. He liked my samples. Our personalities "clicked" and I was hired on the spot.

I've started reviewing gallery shows, theatre, dance and books. I can work from home and don't have to sit in a confining office. I can't believe I'm getting paid to do exactly what I love to do – and getting free tickets besides!

CHAPTER SIXTEEN
THE WHITE-TAILED DEER
(Abundance)

I'd been working for the website for about a year when I decided the time had come to ask for a raise. I hadn't realized, when I started, how many hours the work would actually take. I was usually attending two art shows a week, and two theatre shows. Then I'd spend two or three hours apiece writing them up. In addition, I had to learn HTML and how to use a digital camera. Often there have been publicity photos to pick up, and then I'd have to go into the office to scan them, since I don't have, and can't afford, a scanner of my own. For the amount of work I was doing, I was being highly underpaid.

When I was teaching, I'd never had to ask for a raise. Salaries were determined on a certain predetermined payscale, and increments came automatically – through union negotiations or by piling up education credits. For a shy wordsmith like myself, the whole prospect of promoting myself and talking about that shameful topic called Money was daunting.

I knew my work was good – excellent, in fact; people complimented me on it all the time. But translating my value into dollars and selling the package to the boss was another matter entirely. I realized, too, that once I presented my case I had to be prepared to leave if they turned me down. I couldn't tell them it was impossible for me to live on the low wages they paid me and then hang around. Was I prepared to head for the high road?

I weighed the pros and cons of staying at the job. I liked the "perks"; I liked the presence it gave me in the community. I just couldn't afford to put in so much time for so little money. Perhaps the management believed that at my age, and with the limited number of local media outlets, I had no choice but to remain with them. But people always have choices, I told myself. To explore my options, I returned to the clearing in the woods.

* * *

The light comes through the autumn leaves, making a dappled pattern on the ground. Suddenly, I hear a crackling sound. The bushes part, and there in solemn splendor stands a regal, elegant white-tailed deer, staring at me with great aplomb.

"You are engaged in a battle for survival, I see," the deer observes. "No doubt this is why you have been sent to me." The stag circles around me, sizing me up. "I have known hunger and the fear of hunger," he says. "And now that winter is coming on, I again must scrape and scrounge. Yet I know I will manage. I will not only manage; I will triumph."

"Well, I'm not so sure I will," I complain. "There are so few interesting part time jobs, especially for someone of my age."

"You are operating out of a sense of lack. Your enemy therefore can sense your weakness. You seem unaware that this is a universe of Abundance, and that therefore you are in a position of strength."

"Abundance?"

"Oh, yes. The hunger moon comes, but the hunger moon eventually disappears. And when these woods are sparse, I either remain very still, to save my strength, or move on to forage elsewhere."

"How do you know when it's time to move on?"

"When there is nothing more to be gleaned from the present circumstance."

"I'm not sure I trust the universe to provide."

"Is it that, which has immobilized you?" the deer queries me. "Or is it that you do not trust yourself and your abilities?"

"Maybe both," I reply. "That is, I trust my ability to do good work; I don't trust my ability to get compensated for it."

"What did you do before you did this job which now so troubles you?" the deer asks.

"Most recently, I taught courses at the community college."

"Ah," said the deer. "And is it not possible you could do that once again?"

"Yes," I said. "I can always go back to teaching a course or two. That would give me even more money than I'm making now, and again establish my presence in this community."

"Why did you leave there, may I ask?"

"I was working too hard and felt I was not achieving results. The students were lazy and insolent, and I found it was too frustrating trying to overcome their resistance to learning."

"Was it your job to change them, or to open pathways to knowledge and allow them to follow if they so desired?"

"I guess I took too many of their problems onto myself," I said. "I made myself sick over it."

"Now that you know what you know, however, you could approach the task differently, is that not true?"

"Yes, I suppose I could."

"Must you make an immediate decision?" the deer inquires. "Is it necessary to flee?"

"No, not right away. I need to ask the boss for a raise. And if I don't get it, then I might have to flee."

"Could you not stay where you are and tough it out if you had to?"

"Yes, but not without losing my pride and my sense of worth. It would be as if you hung around the woods without your antlers."

"I see," the deer says. "Not enjoyable. Then it seems to me that before you decide to depart, you must call a meeting with this 'boss' person, and confront him with your demands."

"I am afraid of confrontation," I confess.

"What it is you are afraid of, exactly?"

"That I'll either kill or be killed, I suppose."

"Fighting, for my species, is not about killing," the deer says. "It is about establishing supremacy. It is about defining who has power. My weapon is my set of glorious antlers. What's yours?"

"My talent, I suppose. And my verbal skills."

"Mmm," says the deer. "I have no idea what those are. But you must present your assets in the most positive possible way."

"I'm not sure how," I say. "The head honcho doesn't even know what it is I do."

"Watch me," instructs the deer. He parades up and down, his chest thrust forward, his tail back. "Body language," he says. "Very important."

"I suppose I could marshal my arguments in the best possible light," I consider.

"Good," the deer says. "I don't know what Arguments are, but marshal them, by all means." I take out a piece of paper and make a few notes. "Do you know," continues my interlocutor, "that sometimes we stags practice confrontation before we even meet a competitor?"

"Practice confrontation?"

"Yes. Occasionally I have been known to assault a bush or the trunk of a tree, just to test my strength."

"Are you suggesting I pick fights with strangers, just to keep in shape?"

"No, but if you are seeking this Raise thing, whatever that may be, you might try play-acting your conversation with a friend, presenting your case, perfecting your tone."

This seems like a good idea to me. "Why don't you and I try it right now?" I suggest.

"Very well," the deer agrees. "Pretend I am in my office. You knock. I say come in."

ME: Sir?
DEER: (HIS HEAD DOWN, NOT LOOKING AT ME) Yes? What do you want? I'm very busy.
ME: I want to discuss my future with this company.
DEER: (HE LOOKS UP AND LEANS BACK APPRAISING ME) Um. What about it?
ME: You've often complimented me on my work, said I was the best writer you have. I think I deserve to be making more money. The company is growing. I'd like to grow along with it.
DEER: We don't have regular advertisers for your pages, the way we do for Sports and News. Your pages hardly pay for themselves.

ME: But the arts pages are one of the most attractive features of the site. They draw people in to read the other pages.

DEER: Do they? We don't know that for certain. Now, if you were to go out and get sponsors for your columns, we might have something to discuss.

ME: I'm not a salesperson; I'm a writer. And a very good writer.

DEER: No one's arguing with you about that.

ME: I think I ought to tell you I've been putting in more hours than I thought I would when we agreed on my salary, and I feel I should be reimbursed for all the time I put in.

DEER: Frankly, you waste a lot of time because you don't know computers as well as the rest of us, and everything takes you longer than it needs to.

ME: I'm not a typist, sir, with all due respect. I bring to my work years of experience and knowledge, experience and knowledge that you'd find it difficult to duplicate if I should have to leave.

DEER: Why would you have to leave?

ME: Because I can't afford to live on what you're paying me.

DEER: You're making more than a lot of the other part-time staff.

ME: I'm also older than they are. Most of the geeks are just kids and live at home. I have more expenses than they do.

DEER: I'd hate to see you leave, but we can't afford to pay you any more than we're already paying you. We're expanding into Jacksonville, Orlando, Ocala and Tampa, and we have a lot of cash outlays at present. I'm sorry, but we can't afford a raise for you, and that's that!

ME: Well, thank you for your time. (I HANG MY HEAD AND WALK AWAY)

The deer parades around in a circle and comes back. "Was I all right?" he asks.

"You were perfect," I tell him. "I'm the one who messed up."

"What are you going to do now?"

"If I can't do better than I just did in that encounter, I guess I'll have to leave, and find another job."

"Oh, my," the deer says. "Don't be so hasty. I've asked for many a doe to be my companion, and been turned down. If I gave up right away, our species would have died out long ago. There's something to be said for standing your ground."

"I suppose I could try a different strategy," I muse.

"Why not?" the deer offers. "I shed my antlers every year and grow a brand new set."

Somehow, in the presence of this inspiring creature, I feel more resolute, more capable of dealing with the situation, of trying my best and letting God take care of the results. Still, I do not know how to deal with my intransigent and belittling boss, to get the raise I so badly need.

"You have not given me the answer to my problem," I charge.

"No," says the deer, "but I have given you the tools you will need to solve it yourself. And now, I must be off. It's rutting season, you know."

"Well, I appreciate the time you have taken with me," I begin. Something about him commands respect, and I want him to know it.

"I'm not the most intelligent of animals," the deer admits, "but I am aware of my surroundings, and I am strong."

"I wish I could be as strong as you," I tell him.

"I was not born strong," the deer says. "I made myself strong. When I was a fawn, I ran and jumped and tussled with the other fawns to exercise my muscles and test my endurance. This present situation may be a test for you."

"And if I fail?"

"Then you will learn from your mistakes and go on," says the deer. "Many a buck I know roams the range with a broken antler or a twisted leg. The result of not looking before leaping."

"You are very polite," I compliment him. "It's a pleasure meeting a creature with such fine manners."

"Thank you," says the deer. "I wish you well in all your endeavors." And in a flash he disappears into the thicket, the leaves trembling slightly in his wake.

CHAPTER SEVENTEEN
THE ARMADILLO
(Dealing with Difficult People)

In regard to the raise, I didn't get it. And I couldn't budge the "suit" in charge of business affairs on this issue, even though the Content Manager had promised that he'd put in a good word for me. I threatened to leave, thinking maybe that would startle them into changing their position, but they just said they'd be sorry to see me go. And I didn't really want to go. I liked being an arts reporter, seeing all the new gallery openings in town, getting free tickets to theatre. I enjoyed meeting interesting people through my work, and having a certain status in the community. Then I came up with an idea of how I could keep the job, make more money, and let the "suits" keep their egos intact at the same time.

I agreed to stay on at the same salary, but offered to do book reviews for extra pay. This would not only solve my problem of needing more money, but would put me in closer touch with the literary community in Florida, not to mention supplying me with free books. The Business Manager and the Content Manager took me out to lunch and we discussed it. We had a very pleasant time, and they agreed to my proposal. It was a win-win situation for everybody.

So I stayed on as a freelance arts reporter and loved it, but there was still a really kooky guy, one of the "geeks," the graphic designer, who kept giving me a hard time, throwing a temper tantrum any time I talked to him or came near him. I was also having trouble with a woman at the church, one who was in my circle of krones, who engaged in competitive shouting matches with me in public. I don't respond well to temper tantrums or to go-for-the-jugular verbal battles by invasive individuals. Both remind me too much of my mother.

* * *

"How do you deal with difficult people?" I ask during my next visit to the woods. It is night time, and the place is hushed, except for the distant cacophony of the frogs.

"In my opinion," says a small, squeaky voice, "All people are difficult."

I look around to see where the voice is coming from. There's not a bird, insect or animal anywhere in sight. All I see in front of me is what looks like a roundish rock.

"Well, some are more difficult than others," I answer, mostly to myself. Then a funny little pointed head pokes out from under what I thought was the rock. It's an armadillo.

"You might do well to remember," the armadillo says, "that difficult people are still, in the last analysis, people." He stretches himself out so I can see his lovely plated armor.

I take one look at this weird creature and turn away. "I know, I can see, you don't need to tell me. You're going to say I should develop a shell, and not to let harsh words affect me."

"I wasn't going to say that," the armadillo says, "but it's not a bad idea."

"Well, harsh words do affect me," I let the armadillo know. "I can't help it. I'm sensitive."

"So am I," the armadillo says. "All artists are."

"Don't tell me you're an artist!" I exclaim.

"I've been known to produce a few verses, now and then," the armadillo says shyly.

"Oh, please, recite some for me!" I beg.

"They're all in Spanish," the armadillo says. "But perhaps I can translate a short one for you." He clears his throat and recites:

"Take care! A big monster is coming!
Roll into a ball! Dig a hole!
Hide, hide!
Quiet! The monster is gone.
Your hole is getting deeper.
Stop digging."

"That's very beautiful," I comment. "I'm not sure what it means, but it has a certain music to it."

"It means exactly what it says," the armadillo informs me. "Only more so."

"It seems to be indicating to me that you avoid confrontation. You do not like to do battle."

"On the contrary," the armadillo says. "I often do battle. But when I engage in warfare, I always wear armor."

"Okay, what is my armor?" I ask.

"I don't know," the armadillo says. "How do you usually defend yourself?"

"Sarcasm," I smile.

"That can backfire," the armadillo says.

"It usually does," I acknowledge.

"Rolling into a ball is an excellent device," the armadillo advises. "Just as my poem says."

"I can't do that," I say. "I'm not the same shape you are."

"Figuratively," the armadillo says. "You can look inward and turn off towards the other person. You can let their insults fly off your back."

"And if I cannot?"

"You might try disarming them," the armadillo offers.

"With what?"

"Charm? Humor? Love?"

"That only works with healthy people," I pout. "We're talking about sick people here."

"Ah, sick people. Monsters. Time to dig a hole."

"Wait a minute," I say. "Who made you an expert anyway? I've noticed an awful lot of dead armadillos on the roads of Florida. How do you account for that?"

"We're smart," the armadillo says, "but we're slow. Sometimes we don't get out of the way fast enough."

"But isn't there a certain shame – an admission of defeat – in hiding? In digging a hole? Getting out of the way?"

"It's better than being roadkill," the armadillo says.

"I suppose," I frown.

"Let me ask you this," the armadillo says. "You've engaged in battles with two very aggressive and obnoxious people recently, have you not?"

"I have," I say. "But how did you – "

"It's my business to know these things," the armadillo says. "Now, tell me. Did you win?"

"I might have won the battle," I tell him, "but I feel I lost the war."

"How is that?"

"These people seem to get their kicks from fighting. I feel foolish just having been drawn into their crazy game."

"Why do you have to?"

"I work with them. I have to speak with them."

"If I were you, I would ask myself how necessary it is to have contact with these people, and whether the work could not be accomplished without your paths crossing."

"But – "

"Unless there is a part of you that likes their crazy game."

"No! I hate it!" I declare.

"Well, then," the armadillo says. "You consider whether you really need to be at the same place at the same time that these difficult people are. And you might try rearranging your hours. For example, I prefer being out and about at night. I catch more bugs this way, and I avoid certain – "

"Monsters?"

"Nothing personal," the armadillo says. "But many humans like to make soup out of us."

"Many humans like to make soup out of each other," I observe.

The armadillo raises his eyebrows.

"Figuratively," I add. "We are a rather violent species."

"Ah, yes," the armadillo says. "A species becomes what it practices."

"So you are suggesting – ?"

"Practice peace." The armadillo smiles serenely and waddles slowly away.

* * *

It turned out I was not the only one who had trouble communicating with our moody and irritable graphic designer at work. He'd had stormy words with numerous people, screaming that he was under too much stress. In order to contain his rages, the administration finally moved him into his own carpeted office. After that, our paths rarely crossed at all, and if I needed anything from him, I requested it by e-mail.

As for my contentious friend at the church – I resigned from the committee we were on together, and joined another committee (change of place and time, as the armadillo suggested). And then one day the friend came up to me at church and said, in her stentorian tone, "I don't have a sister, so why don't you be my sister, and then we can fight all the time?"

"I do have a sister," I responded. "And fighting is not what being a sister is about." And then, I suppose I mentally rolled myself into a ball, but I found myself saying, "Would you do me a huge favor, and never speak to me again?"

"Never?" the woman gasped.

"Never," I smiled.

She has complied, and there are no more occasions for unnecessary battles.

No longer needing to retreat, I have stopped digging.

CHAPTER EIGHTEEN
THE SPIDER
(Love versus Control)

"Sweet are the uses of adversity," wrote Shakespeare. If it weren't for the troubles I'd been having, I might not have fallen in love. Let me try to recall how my love affair started. The woman and ex-friend who had given me so much flak at the church did not let go easily. She began an e-mail campaign against me, sending vicious communications to everyone we both knew, but especially powerful figures such as the minister and friends who were published and successful writers who might possibly be helpful to me. The men we knew seemed to be egging us on, eager to witness a "cat fight" – until I put a stop to the whole thing by reminding them that computers came with a "delete" key and that I would use it for any e-mail from this "lady" and from any friends who wished to fan the flames of disagreement.

Sunday at the church was difficult for me, and I was totally stressed out. A sweet young man in his forties, with red hair and a red beard had been sitting next to me. He seemed a bit of a loner, stood aloof after the service, smoking unfiltered cigarettes. So I went up and spoke to him. He was quiet, but intelligent, and seemed a good listener. I confided in him about a personality clash I was having and how much it bothered me that people seemed to enjoy watching a fight. He told me I needed to relax.

"How would you like to come with me for a small adventure?" he asked. He had said the magic word: Adventure. He drove me down to his house near Panacea (magical name!) and we went walking barefoot in the sand. We recognized that we were kindred souls – individualists, non-conformists. He said he liked older women, and that he'd never been married and never wanted to get married, because he did not want children. The following week, we went swimming at a peaceful, isolated lake where there was no one except us and the wild birds. He had begun to replace my stressful memories with beautiful ones. He took me to places I had only been to in dreams.

But he made me feel insecure. Correction. I felt insecure. The age difference. The fact that he hated to make plans, but just liked to "drop in." The fact that he was handsome and sexy and had a wandering eye. I wanted a committed relationship from him. He would not agree to one.

Confused, and yet drawn increasingly closer to him, I decided to meditate about it. I wanted to know how I could capture him completely, how I could hold him and make him mine for a long, long time.

* * *

In the forest of my mind, I see an intricate spider web, glistening with dew. And soon, I see the female spider, putting the finishing touches to her handiwork.

"Madame," I begin.

"Yes?" She looks at me with a sidelong glance, and then creates a rope for herself to shimmy down, so she can come converse with me.

"You know how to weave a web, to attract, entice and entrap," I observe.

"Yes," she replies.

"I want to do the same," I propose.

"Do you?" she responds.

"I think I am in love with someone," I confess. "And I don't want him to just come and go as he pleases."

"Don't you?" she says. I'm beginning to think she is incapable of sentences longer than two words.

"No," I tell her. "He's good, you see. He's very good. He's bright and generous and kind. And he's wonderful in bed."

"So?" she goes.

"So I want him with me all the time," I explain.

"Why?" she asks.

"Because he's fun," I tell her.

"Ah," she says. "Mating is enjoyable, is it not?"

"Oh, yes," I cry. At last I seem to be getting through to her. "It's very enjoyable indeed!"

"Does he think you are beautiful?" she asks.

"He tells me so."

"They always tell me I am beautiful," the spider says.

"You are!" I flatter her. "For a spider, that is!"

"Miss Muffet did not think so," the spider recalls.

"What did she know?" I cajole. "Anybody on a diet of curds and whey – "

"So you wish me to tell you my secret?" she asks. "The secret of how to make sure a male will never leave you?"

"Yes, yes!" I cry.

"First," she drawls, "I attract him."

"Yes?" I encourage her. "How do you do that?"

"Every way I can," she says. "I make myself irresistible."

"Go on."

"Then," she continues, "I hold him in my arms."

"How romantic!" I sigh.

"It's easier when you have eight legs, the way I do," she says.

"I don't think I could attract him if I had eight legs," I tell her.

"Perhaps not," she says. "We engage in elaborate courtship rituals. I invite him to dinner. I feed him with my mouth. I massage his back."

"I've done that," I say.

"We engage in exciting, passionate sex."

"And then?"

"And then, I kill him and I devour him."

"What?"

"You wanted to know how you could make sure he would never leave you."

"But – "

"How you could always remain in control."

"Yes, but that's pretty drastic – "

"You will have to choose, my dear. Those are the rules. You will have to decide: Do you want Love or do you want Control? The two never go together."

"I was hoping you would tell me."

"Do you humans learn nothing from your experience?" the spider asks. "You have just lost a woman friend. Why? Because instead of letting you be who you are, she attempted to control you."

"She was," I have to agree, "A domineering b ---- "

"Now, now," the spider cautions. "No need to let her transgressions divert you from being a lady."

"Sorry," I apologize.

"She has no boyfriends, does she?" the spider probes.

"No, come to think of it, she does not. She kept company for awhile with an alcoholic."

"A control game if ever there was one," the spider comments. "Is that what you want?"

"No!" I declare. "I was married to an alcholic. He expected me to control him, but I didn't want to."

"The point is, you do not like being drawn into someone else's game of control. What makes you think your young man would like it?"

"He wouldn't have to know about it," I suggest.

"Then he would be mighty stupid," she says. "And yours is not stupid. He is open and honest. And he loves freedom."

"But you yourself have chosen the other path," I remind her.

"I never said you should copy my way of life," the spider says. "I have made my choice; you must make yours."

"I suppose you're right," I say. "My sister chose as you did. She has absolute control over her husband, control she achieves through her hypochondria and complaining. And they haven't had any sex in twelve years."

"There you go," the spider says.

"And I raised my son without controlling him," I muse. "We love and respect each other now, and have become more than mother and son; we are friends."

"You see?"

"But this Love business – I mean Romance – it's so precarious, it's so unpredictable, so scary!"

"That's what makes it interesting, isn't it?" the spider grins.

"I suppose."

The spider begins to laugh, a raucous, cackling laugh.
"What's so funny?" I ask.
"A fly is caught in my web. He looks so helpless! He hasn't a clue!"

I look at the arachnid with fear and aversion. Compassion seems completely lacking in her. She begins to shimmy up the cord she has created for herself.

"But how will it all end?" I call after her.
"When you choose Love, you never know!" she calls back. "Just enjoy him, while you can!"

CHAPTER NINETEEN
THE FROG
(Unlucky in Love)

For several months I was on Cloud Nine. My boyfriend took me for thrilling rides on the back of his motorcyle; we went to concerts and theatre together, and on beautiful nature walks, where he pointed out the fauna and flora of his native Florida. He was a sweet, gentle lover, and he made me feel good about my body. Then he dumped me in favor of a prettier, younger woman. She happened to be a friend of mine (he met her at a party at my house!) and who went to the same church fellowship. I tried speaking to my best friend about it, and she made light of the whole thing: How could it be a serious relationship when he was so much younger? It saddened me that she could not see how deep my feelings were and how much I was hurting. It's an age-old story; it's happened thousands of times before. But when it happens to you, it feels like the world is coming to an end.

I needed peace of mind in peaceful surroundings, and so I went in my mind to a grassy bank at the edge of a small lake. There were grebes and blue herons wading there, a snowy egret and a regal anhinga, spreading its wings in the sun. I wondered which of these was going to be my guide, to help me find my way back to healing.

* * *

I close my eyes, breathe deeply, and then hear a metallic voice saying, "For-give it, for-give it, for-give it!" I am in the company of a large green frog, who has jumped out of the lake to come give me counsel. He is wearing a golfer's outfit, with a jaunty cap on his head.

"How can I forgive what he has done to me?" I cry. "He was cruel; he abused me; he trivialized our relationship! I want to make him realize that what he did was wrong, that I don't deserve the treatment he gave me!"

"Him, him, him, – hum, hum, hum," the frog

"I beg your pardon? What's that supposed to mean?"

"You need to take the focus off of him, and put it onto yourself."

"Myself," I mumble. "My self-esteem is in the pits. I feel as helpless, weak and vulnerable as a – well, a tadpole!"

"I know," the frog says, peering at me with his huge, lidded eyes. "But you can go through a metamorphosis, like I did, and make yourself into the creature you want to be. The creature which will attract whatever it is you want to attract."

"I feel," I went on, wallowing in self pity just awhile longer, "that I've had an arm or a leg cut off."

"I know the feeling," the frog commiserates. "I've had it happen. I also know that an arm or leg can grow back again in my case, or be sewed on again in yours. Your indispensable partner can be replaced. And will be."

"So where do I begin?" I ask, "Putting my self esteem back together?"

"You can't stay where you are," the frog says. "You'll drown in crocodile tears. Do you know what I do, when the lilypad I'm sitting on begins to sink?"

"No, what?"

"I hop to another lilypad," he says.

"All my lilypads are sinking," I moan.

"Come on," the frog says. "I bet there are a few things you are good at. What is it that you do well?"

"I don't know. What do you do well?"

"I'm so glad you asked," the frog says. He begins blowing up his gills until they look like bright pink balloons. "There!" he chortles. "Bet you can't do that!"

"I have some abilities," I admit, "Like speaking French and playing tennis. But I'm not terribly good at them."

"Well, then," says the frog. "There's a project for you. Why not become better at them? Take a class. Get in some practice. Restore your confidence."

"Why do you do that thing with your gills anyway?" I ask.

"Those are not gills, they are vocal sacks," the frog corrects me. They enable my adorable voice to resonate so that I may issue forth my mating calls. If you came back here on a spring night, the lake would be crowded with many different kinds of gentlemen frogs and toads, all performing their delightful croaking calls to attract females."

"I've heard the chorus of frogs at night," I recall. "But how does it help you, when all the male frogs are beeping their signals at the same time?"

"The calls may sound the same to you, but they're quite unique to us. They enable us to find partners of our own species, because each species has a very special mating call. I dare say this person you are lamenting the loss of, comes from the same species that you do?"

"I'm not so sure," I reply. "We're of different religious backgrounds, come from different parts of the country, have completely different interests. And he's been diagnosed manic-depressive."

"And this is what attracted you?"

The frog is making me think, – about why I get attracted to men who are wrong for me – and I don't really want to think right now. I want to wallow in muck. "No, that's not what attracted me," I respond with annoyance. "I thought I could change him."

"Kiss him and turn him into a prince, as the fable goes?" the frog smiles knowingly.

"Well, yes, if you put it that way."

"I have inhabited this lake for nearly five years," the frog tells me in a stern tone of voice. "Underwater and on the land. And I have never yet seen a frog turn into a prince. Never happened, never will." He sticks out his tongue and catches an insect. Then he proceeds to croak until he hears a response from the other side of the lake. He winks at me. "I think she's my type," he says. "I wonder if she plays golf."

"Those sacks make you look a lot bigger than you actually are," I note.

"Ah, yes, that's another thing that makes me a hit with the ladies. I find you always have to puff yourself up a bit when you first meet someone."

"Yeah," I grouse. "She puffs herself up quite a bit."

"You are not to speak of her any more," the frog orders me. "Nor of him. And do not speak to them, if you can possibly help it. Doing so will only prolong your pain."

"I need to lose weight," I comment.

"You're fine the way you are." I remember I'm talking to one of the world's ugliest looking creatures. Yet he's contented and thinks very highly of himself. Perhaps that's because he concentrates on what he does do well.

"What creative projects are you working on right now?" he asks.

"Oh, I'm too broken-hearted to be creative right now," I reply.

"That's bad," he says. "All creatures were born to be creative, to lay many eggs which will hatch into new ideas. Creativity is essential to your health.

"Aren't you exaggerating?" I scoff.

"Certainly not," he answers. "'That talent which is death to hide,'" said Keats of his poetry. Let me warn you, if you call a halt to your natural creativity, you will get sick and die."

"You make everything sound so easy," I say. "Can't you see, I'm in pain? I guess you've never been rejected by someone you loved."

"Oh, haven't I?" the frog says. "I courted Miss Beatrice all last spring, and she would have none of me. But, there's lots of frogs in the pond, as they say. I'm simply too busy to mope."

"You think that's what I'm doing? Moping?"

"Most definitely," asserts the frog. It's time for you to get back to the process of Creation. Create art, create light, create a better world, but most important of all, create yourself."

My green companion whistles a few bars of "Mr. Froggie Went A-Courtin'," as if to make me realize that in the frog world, he's quite the sport.

* * * * *

Later, in a book I am reading about Mythology, I come across the following:

"Frogs are associated with the Creation myths in several ancient cultures. The Egyptians believed that the frog-headed goddess Heket, together with her husband Khnumu, created mankind. The people of China and India had a legend that the world rested on the back of a giant frog, and that earthquakes and tremors were the result of his movements. In Central America, the Mayan Indians believed that the croaking of frogs brought the rain that watered the crops, and linked frogs to fertility and birth."

CHAPTER TWENTY
DR. RABBIT
(No Place Like Home)

I have had the same recurring dream – more like a nightmare – for many years. In it, I am voyaging far from home, in Canada, or Europe or another city, and something happens – either I lose my luggage, my purse, my son (who is always a child in my dreams), my map, my tickets – and I can't get home again. Each time I have this dream I think, "Well, now I've explored all the permutations of this subject, and I never need to have the dream again," and then another permutation comes along; I'm walking down strange streets, and I'm stranded far away from friends, family and the familiar environment where I belong.

I have not had good luck with psychotherapists, most of whom seem to believe that dreams only have one meaning. They use them to promote their own agendas. I believe that dreams are like poems, full of metaphors that explode into many meanings.

Perhaps, I ponder, it is time to meditate about this, to ask my inner therapist what this dream is all about, so that I can stop having it for once and for all. I go in my mind to a field of daisies at the edge of my favorite woods, and request an interview with an imaginary therapist, whom I shall call Dr. Mischa Goss.

What appears before me, poking her long furry ears out of a hole, is a greyish-brown lady rabbit.

"Sorry to inform you," she says to me, in a soft, comforting voice, "that Dr. Goss just had a nervous breakdown, one of the hazards of our profession, so they sent me instead. You can just call me Beth."

"Doesn't that mean 'house' in Hebrew?" I ask.

"It most certainly does," she replies, twitching her nose with glee. "How clever of you to know that."

"It's about the word 'house' I wish to speak with you," I tell the rabbit. "Or more exactly, the word 'home.'"

"What about the word 'home'?" she asks, and she stretches out on the grass, perking her ears up to listen. I'm very glad she has not asked me to lie down, because I recall this being a major issue when I tried going to a real therapist, and I didn't want to spend the time on that issue again.

I tell her the dream, in its latest form. This time it's Toronto, but it doesn't matter where I go; what matters is that I can't find my way back.

"I see," she says. "Tell me. What does the word 'home' mean to you?"

"It could be many things," I begin. "It could be my body, the place where I live."

"Do you have health problems?" she inquires.

"I did," I told her. "I am in remission from cancer. There's always the hidden fear that I could have a recurrence."

"What else?"

"It could be my home page on the Web, which is also my place of employment. But I've had this dream many years before I started working for the website I work for now."

"Why don't you free-associate with the word. I'll write down everything you say." She sits up and produces a small pad and pencil from her vest, and begins to take notes.

"Okay," I agree. "Home truths, comforts of home, home is where the heart is, there's no place like home, broken home, you can't go home again, home cooking, hearth and home, keep the home fires burning, nobody's home."

"Good, very good" she says. "Now, have you considered the possibility that you're dealing with the literal meaning of the word? The place where you reside?"

"I thought it would be more complicated than that," I say.

"Perhaps it is," she says, "but why don't we start there. Tell me how you feel about your home, the place where you live, past and present."

"I never felt at home in my parents' home," I begin.

"Why not?" she asks me.

"It was theirs," I reminisce. "It never felt like mine. I didn't feel I really belonged there, that they really wanted me or loved me."

"Did you have no possessions of your own?" she asked.

"No, come to think of it, I didn't," I frown. "My parents didn't give me toys, didn't allow me to decorate my own room. The living room was all in my mother's taste – with her color scheme of chartreuse and red – and I hated it. The people who came to visit were their friends; I had none of my own."

"Go on," she says.

"When I was married, we owned a house, but that never was a home either, because my husband used it like a hotel and was hardly ever there."

"Pity," comments Beth.

"And then after my divorce, we traveled around a lot, lived in temporary quarters." I continue.

"You have a feeling of being temporary," she summarizes.

"Yes," I say. "Of not belonging anywhere."

"And where you are living now?"

"I own my own home, but I still don't feel comfortable there," I tell her. "I'm not happy in the neighborhood where I am now. My friends don't like to come there because they don't feel their cars will be safe. And I was robbed the first year I was there, so whenever I go out, I wonder if I'll come back and interrupt another burglary."

"Shall I tell you how I feel about my home?" the rabbit asks.

"Yes, please do," I urge her.

"My home," says the rabbit, "is a place of warmth and safety. I have many enemies – weasels, and foxes, badgers and buzzards, hawks and owls – but when I am home, I am in a place I have created for myself where I can relax and be myself."

"You live in a burrow, as I recall," I say.

"Quite so," she says. "And since I love companionship, my neighbors and I often join our burrows into what we call a 'warren.' It's what you might call an apartment house, or a community."

"Community," I echo. "That's part of it. That's something I feel I'm missing. But doesn't it get awfully crowded where you live?"

"When it's time to have babies," she explains, "and I do love to have babies – I build us a nest."

"A nest," I repeat again. "Perhaps what I'm feeling is a nesting instinct."

"I keep my nest very clean," the rabbit goes on. "Never litter it, never foul the nest with droppings. Always excrete outside – twice, as a matter of fact. First, soft pellets which I ingest and then excrete again as hard pellets, which mingle with the earth. I like to have pleasant, attractive surroundings."

"So do I!" I exclaim.

"And do you?"

I am embarrassed to admit that I have not paid much attention to fixing up my abode, and it's usually pretty messy.

"Why don't you keep it nicer?" she asks.

I tell her I'm not sure, but maybe I still can't believe I'm in a place that's truly mine. And also, it's a lot of work, keeping up a house all by myself. I can't get anyone to mow the lawn, or to fix things when they are broken. It's expensive to keep hiring repairmen, and I resent the money I have to spend just to prevent the place from falling apart. I want to use that money for travel.

"If you are not comfortable where you are," the rabbit says, "Why don't you move?"

"I've thought of that," I tell the rabbit. "But I've moved so often. And it's such a hassle."

"Don't you want a place that is really yours? A place that expresses who you really are?"

"Yes, I do," I say plaintively. I tell her that I keep losing my keys, she is of the opinion that I am telling myself it is time to move on.

"But if I sell the house, where will I go?" I ask.

"Why don't you try to visualize that?" the rabbit asks me. She informs me that Visualization is a form of Prayer. She asks me to describe my perfect home.

I picture an apartment, not a house, right in the center of town. It has a fireplace in the living room, and no lawns to mow, but a patio in back, with flowers. It is sunny and light and spacious, with walk-in closets. It is in a safe neighborhood. It is cozy and comfortable. My friends feel at ease there, and so do I.

"Good," she says. "Now, you remember that. Would you like to come visit my digs?"

I thank her, but decline the offer. It seems to me that *Alice in Wonderland* began that way, and I'm in no mood for such an adventure. But I make a mental note that I want to have a place to live where I'll be proud to say, "Would you like to come visit my digs?"

* * * * *

I put my house on the market, with a real estate agent I'd met at a spiritual seminar. She turned out to be a worldbeater of an agent, who made several suggestions for sprucing up my house so that it appealed to buyers. I steam-cleaned the driveway, bought hanging flowerpots for the front of the house, cleared the weeds out of the backyard. The place looked so charming I almost wanted to stay there myself. It sold in two weeks. Then I went into a complete panic, because I had to be out of the place by the end of the month, and I had no place to go.

"You will find the right place," the agent told me. "Why don't you try Visualization?" I swear she twitched her nose when she said that.

I went back and looked at my Visualization list again. And the following week, answering an ad in the paper, I walked into a duplex townhouse and saw every one of the features I'd listed for my imaginary dream house. There was a fireplace and a patio, two huge bedrooms upstairs, one of which I could use as a studio. The neighborhood was quiet and peaceful, but within walking distance of Lake Ella, the senior center, the library, and downtown.

I have been living here now for almost two years. I feel comfortable and contented here. I like my neighbors. The adjoining townhouses remind me of a warren. And I haven't had that recurring dream since I moved in.

CHAPTER TWENTY-ONE
THE TURTLE DOVE
(Finding a Life Partner)

In my special place under a tree at the edge of the wood, I have spread a blanket and am about to take a nap in the warmth of the sun, when I am aware of a gentle cooing sound. I look to the top of the tree and see a pair of turtle doves. What a provident opportunity, I think, to interview a "lovebird," about my goal of finding a lifelong mate.

The female bird is building a nest with her partner. She is busy weaving twigs, when I call up to her, "Hello!"

"Hello!" she answers back. "What can I dooooo for youuuuu?

"I have been sent to you, or you have been sent to me," I begin, "so that you might answer a question for me."

"I hope it's not a hard one," the lovebird says. "I don't have an encyclopedic mind. I'm a rather physical creature, and think in terms of practical, empirical solutions to simple, everyday problems."

"Exactly what I need," I encourage her. "What I want to know is, How can I find a loving partner who will want to nest with me for keeps?"

Not having the time nor the inclination for lengthy palaver, the bird sums it up in three words: "Nest, Plumage, Song."

I try to barrage her with follow-up questions, but she simply continues building her house, cocking one eye at me as if to say, "You figure it out. I've given you the keys, now open the doors."

Starting backwards, something that contrarian Arians are wont to do, I realize I've never had much trouble in the Song department. In fact, that has been my primary area of concentration my whole life. I have polished my verses, sometimes even published them. But still, the male of the species, if he will listen at all, simply says, "That's nice," and flies away.

Question: Is it that I'm singing my own song, and not his? Conveying the wrong calls to the right party and/or the right calls to the wrong party? Whippoorwills don't respond to words meant for robins, etc. Birds are instinctively born with their calls. We must, therefore, (a) learn what type we are, what kind of lifestyle we prefer, what sort of trees we like to live in, how high we like to fly, and with whom. Only then can we find "birds of a feather." (b) Once we identify ourselves and our needs, we must fashion ways of communicating who we are to creatures similar to ourselves.

I did get married once, but to the wrong person. That's because I sent out signals which were highly effective (I blush to think what tricks I employed!) but I did not know what I was really like, so I was just like a mocking bird – aping the cries of everyone else, but not having a distinctive pattern of my own. That would have been fine if I cared to continue life as a mockingbird, but I really wished to fly like an eagle. This made me very dissatisfied, and my mockingbird husband very nervous.

Now I think I know myself better, and what my needs are, and I'm working on finding the right note, the keynote, as it were, to bring suitors flocking around.

Plumage is a recent discovery for me. My mother always told me clothes were unimportant; it was "character" that counted. That's because she never wanted to spend any money on my wardrobe. Also, she was extremely jealous of her daughters and wanted to play them down as much as possible, dressing us in hand-me-downs and ill-fitting garments.

Anyway, through a process of trial and error, I have found what looks well on me. I am now able to attract any type of male. However, they do not stick around long. This brings me to the third item, which is the one the dove mentioned first: Nest.

To me, that means a long-term live-in situation. Concentrating on obtaining sexual fulfillment has netted me zilch. I'm simply not temperamentally suited for casual affairs, and that's all I seem to get. The only satisfying sexual relationship I ever had was when I lived with a man for two years, and set up housekeeping with him. It did not continue because he was not the person I wanted to marry – I did not respect him enough – but I did let him know, as soon as we met, that I was looking for someone to live with.

What prevents a man from leaving his wife, even when other factors in their relationship are not compatible? The comfort of his home. Witness the long-term marriages in my family, where the couple has not had sex for years and scarcely spends any time together. Witness also the successful children's book writer I met, who has affairs but who can't leave home, because that's his studio and it would upset his routine. What makes a man think "Marriage," when he starts dating a woman, and not "Temporary affair"?

Just before I got married, I had a very small apartment, but it was in an upscale neighborhood, and I kept it neat. I also began decorating his apartment for him. This was one of my tricks. I knew that every time he turned on the lamp I'd bought him, he'd think of me.

The lovebird suggests that if I am not comfortable in my home, nobody else will be. The male of the species makes a note of the female's surroundings, to see if she is capable of giving him a place where he will want to stay.

The lovebirds begin cooing at each other again. The female comes down, perches in front of me, and says it's a pity that I'm too large to come visit them in their nest. She loves having company, she says, and asks me if I feel the same.

I frown, and realize that my home is currently set up just for me. The apartment I have now is sunny, spacious and elegant, but there is also something transient and un-cozy about it. Maybe because it's only <u>worked</u> in, and not <u>lived</u> in. I begin thinking of ways to make it a more welcoming space, and I make the following list.

MAKING MY HOUSE A HOME

(1) Clean the place thoroughly and keep it clean.

(2) Cozy it up as much as possible, with more comfortable seating.

(3) Make the place reflect my interests – artwork, books, fine dining.

(4) Keep fresh flowers on the table.

(5) Invite people in at least once a week, to give it warmth. In *The Sayings of the Fathers,* a book of Jewish wisdom, there is a saying, "Beware of the person who has weeds growing over the path to his door."

CHAPTER TWENTY-TWO
THE RED FOX
(Affirmations on Lovability)

"I want to be pretty," I tell the universe. "I want to remarry. Where can I find a good man?"

"Where, indeed!" barks the sprightly red fox, who appears to me in my next meditation.

"You animals have a bag of tricks," I mutter enviously. "Scent and coloring, mating rituals – "

"Don't forget our beautiful tails!" the vixen says, swishing hers around most immodestly. The way I was raised, I was warned not to brag, not to show off. But this lady seems to do both, with great effect.

"I want to be foxy, like you," I declare.

"And what's preventing you?" she asks.

This question gives me pause for a moment. "I've been rejected so many times," I recollect. "It's made me feel unworthy and unwanted."

"It hasn't made you feel anything," the fox corrects me. "You are the only one in control of your feelings."

"All right, I have allowed myself to feel unworthy and unwanted, after so many rejections," I amend.

"That's more like it," the fox says, batting her eyes at me.

"You have very beautiful eyes," I compliment her.

"So do you," the fox says. "So does everybody. But you don't use yours for anything but reading, do you?"

"Beg pardon?"

"Eyes," the fox whispers to me, getting so close I can feel the texture of her fine fur and the warmth of her breath, "as Shakespeare said, 'are the windows of the soul.' And they are wonderful for flirting!"

"What is flirting, exactly?" I ask. "I never did learn to flirt."

"Impossible!" the fox cries. "Didn't you ever watch your mother flirting with your father?"

"That's part of the problem," I lament. "My mother just yelled at and criticized my father. I never saw any positive interaction between them."

"Hmmm," the fox says. "But surely you must have picked up something – "

"Oh yes. When my mother was around men, she would raise her voice a few octaves, to a silly, childish squeak, and she would make mistakes on purpose in what she was saying, so that men would correct her. I found the whole act a bit appalling."

"So would I," the fox agrees. "That's not flirting; that's controlling."

"Then what is flirting?"

"It's showing them everything you've got," the fox grins, "And then not giving them anything."

"I see," I say, totally confused.

"You're totally confused, aren't you!" the fox smiles. She's good at reading minds.

"Yes," I confess. "I just don't get it. The whole thing seems like just a silly game."

"A game, yes," the fox concurs. "But not silly at all." She admires herself in a small puddle and preens her forepaws. "Do you not enjoy The Chase?" she asks, glancing at me sideways.

"The Chase?"

"Oh, yes!" she giggles gleefully, "He chases you until you catch him."

"What's enjoyable about it?" I want to know.

"Everything!" she replies. "The thrill of the hunt, the mystery of hide-and-seek! It calls upon your powers of invention!"

"Ah." I consider this for a moment. "But let's say I did by some miracle become terribly attractive and have men following after me in droves. What then? What if I had all sorts of horrible men on my trail, bothering me and bullying me and blasting my peace of mind – "

"Ah, now we're getting down to it," the fox says. She curls up on a bed of dried leaves, and looks at me with her head resting on her paws. "You're afraid of attracting the wrong kind."

"Why, yes, aren't you?"

"I often have attracted the wrong kind," she acknowledges. "Packs of dogs. And human beings – or those who call themselves human beings – who come after me with guns, wanting not to love me, but to kill me."

"And what do you do about that?" I inquire.

"Lead them a merry chase," the fox answers. "Take them on false trails. Run them around in circles until they get tired out. But the best thing you can do is not be home."

"Not be home?"

"Have you heard of something called a foxhole?"

"Yes, it's sometimes used in war."

"Right. And when evil people come after you, then it is war. So what I do sometimes is dig a hole and crawl in. You needn't be afraid, you see. You always have the ability – and the right – to say no."

"I guess I'm afraid I won't be able to tell, who's evil and who's not."

"Eyes and ears, my dear." The fox cautions. "That's what God gave them to us for. You start looking for clues the minute they enter your territory."

"Clues?"

"Oh, yes!" the fox says. "That's another thing that makes the game so exciting! It's like being a detective!"

"I never looked at it that way," I admit. I picture myself in a Sherlock Holmes outfit. "And what if I don't like the clues I'm picking up?"

"I don't know about your species," the fox says. "But it is canine canon to set boundaries."

"We don't do that the way you do," I point out. "So we have a great number of folks who don't recognize or respect boundaries."

"Snarl. Growl. Chase them off," she shrugs.

I practice growling. The fox throws back her head and laughs. "You are a funny one!" she says.

"What do you mean?" I frown.

"Here you are worried about how you're going to get rid of men, when you haven't even figured out how you're going to attract them!"

"You're making me feel pretty darn foolish," I tell her.

"I'm good at that," the fox says.

"Are you going to get around to answering my original question?" I challenge.

"What was the question again? I forget." I am positive, from the look on her face, that she has not forgotten at all.

"Where can I find a good man?"

"Let me turn the question around and ask it of you. Where *can* you find a good man?"

"Anywhere," I realize.

"Quite so!" says the fox. "If you're in the right mood. A confident mood, a playful mood."

"And how do you suggest I get there?"

"I'll tell you what I tell my cubs," the vixen says. "Nothing succeeds like success. I'm sure you've heard that before. Start building little success experiences for yourself."

"I'd love to," I say. "But how?"

"The way my cubs do. They practice by playing."

"Playing?"

"Through play, they learn to be affectionate. They tease each other, they engage in mock battles. Then they learn to hunt for small game. They play the field."

"Play the field."

"Flirt with every male you see. Until you find one who wishes to mate for life."

"But they might get the wrong idea – " I begin.

"Oh, but you must make it clear what it is you want, sweet thing," she says. "You must make it clear that you also wish to mate for life. That is how I found my Prince Charming."

"The confidence part," I say. "That's the hardest part for me."

"Do you do affirmations?" the fox asks.

"I used to," I respond.

"Did they work?"

"Why, yes, they did. I don't know why I stopped."

"Perhaps because you got what you wanted. Now, if you can picture the kind of mate you want, you must affirm your ability to get him."

"Oh, dear," I cry. "I don't even know how to begin! I've been out of the ratrace for so long."

"It's not a ratrace," the fox says, "Unless you are looking for a rat."

"No!" I contradict her. "I'm looking for a kind, healthy, loving man who is able and willing to support me in all my endeavors, as I will support him in his."

"That's a start," the fox says. "Now try these. You might even want to write them down:

'I am a magnet'

'I am desirable'

'I am loving and lovable'

'I attract someone who meets my physical, mental, and emotional needs'"

She stops and looks at me searchingly. "Do you notice what these phrases have in common?" she asks.

"They're all in the present tense," I observe.

"Precisely," she approves. "Ever notice how fast I can run? Ever wonder how I can get where I want to go with such speed and alacrity?"

"What's your secret?" I ask.

"I don't carry any baggage with me," she says. "Present tense. Notice anything else about my affirmations?"

"There are no negative words in them. No 'I will not's."

"Excellent," the fox says. "Go to the head of your class. There are enough obstacles in the real world – brooks and stones and fallen tree limbs – without your having to create obstacles for yourself to jump over."

I get out a piece of paper and start writing down affirmations. The fox looks over my shoulder. "By Jove, I think she's got it!" she says, quoting *My Fair Lady*. She starts to slink away, then comes back.

"One more thing," she says.

"Yes?"

"Don't forget to smile!" And with a smile that could charm the birds off the trees, and often has, she is gone, leaving me looking forward to my next encounter with a male of the species, and a chance to once again start playing The Game.

CHAPTER TWENTY-THREE
THE SALAMANDER
(Dumping a Bad Habit)

I gave up smoking over a year ago. But this week, with all the tension in my life – a lover leaving me, the denial of my raise, worry about money – I am sorely tempted to resume the habit, or at least, to buy a pack, as if it would provide solace and friendship not found elsewhere. To fight the inclination, I breathe deeply, close my eyes, and find myself once again in the meditation space, under a tree in the woods.

There appears, scampering towards me on a log, a green salamander. He tells me he is a reincarnation of Socrates.

"Yeah, sure," I respond. "And I'm the Queen of Sheba."

"You don't have to believe me if you don't want to," the salamander says. "But I'd prefer it if we do not sit under a hemlock tree."

"Why do I suddenly want to go back to smoking?" I appeal to him.

"I'll ask the questions, if you don't mind," the salamander smiles. "For unlike wise people like you, I know how ignorant I am, and therefore I must attain wisdom by asking questions."

"Whatever works," I concede.

"Smoking is a bad habit, you will agree?" the salamander posits.

"It certainly is. Gives you cancer, makes your breath stink, and it's expensive."

"Then why, knowing it is bad, do people do it anyway?"

"It's a habit, it's an addiction –" I begin.

"There must be some good in the bad habit, then, mustn't there?" the salamander proceeds.

"Yes, it's comforting. At least for the time that the cigarette is in my mouth or in my hand."

"Can there be no other sources of comfort?" the salamander asks.

"Oh, yes, plenty," I say. "But not as readily available, perhaps."

"So, you smoke because of tension?" the salamander inquires.

"Yes. Crises. Of which I experience around ten or a dozen a day."

"Or situations which you perceive as crises. Tell me, are human beings animals?"

"Depends on how you define 'animals.'"

"Living beings distinguished from plants because of their capability for spontaneous movement?"

"Well, if you put it that way – I suppose we are animals. Mammals. Homo sapiens. Homo erectus. Home on the Range."

"Do you ever see other animals puffing on cigarettes?"

"Can't say I have," I reply. "Except maybe Joe Camel. And he's a mythical beast."

"Yet is it not true that animals suffer from tension and crises as well as humans do?"

"Maybe even more," I concur.

"Then why is it we do not smoke?"

"You haven't discovered fire yet?"

"Wrong answer!" the salamander snaps. He's beginning to question whether he has actually mastered the art of asking questions. "Oh, we could light fires if we wanted to," he insists. "Some of us do, in fact. Fireflies. Electric eels."

"I'm talking cooking fires," I pursue. "Like in stoves, forges and furnaces. Our control over carbonization has put us at the top of the food chain."

"Where you won't remain long," the salamander snickers, "if you insist on burning substances which give you cancer."

"If you're going to take a moralistic approach," I threaten, "I'm outa here. I don't feel I have control over the smoking. It has control over me."

"Smoking, then, is not a rational decision?"

"I don't think so. I've seen all the scientific literature about what it does to the lungs, and while I read the articles I was puffing away on a cigarette."

"If it is not a rational activity, it must then be an irrational one?"

"Well, duh, I guess so."

"Would it not make sense, then, to approach its cessation of this habit from a non-logical, purely physical point of view?"

"Probably," I reflect. "But I'm not sure how."

"The next time a crisis comes along, or a high-stress situation, instead of lighting a cigarette, why not do something else?"

"Such as?"

"Would you like to know how I deal with stress?"

"I am eager to find out," I say. I think I remember Plato saying that once to his teacher.

"I take naps. I lie in the sun. I breathe deeply. I find alternative coping mechanisms. I take a walk, go for a swim."

"But I'm a worrier," I say. "I worry a lot."

"Do you find that worrying about something that might happen has any positive effect on the outcome?"

"None whatsoever," I acknowledge.

"That in actuality, you are going through a dangerous or threatening or unpleasant situation twice? Once in reality and once beforehand, in your mind?"

"More than twice," I agree.

"Are you aware that I am capable of regenerating a lost limb or tail?" the salamander asks me.

"I believe I heard that somewhere."

"This knowledge aids me in my relaxed attitude. Do you not believe that confidence in your regenerative capabilities might enhance your ability to relax?"

"Possibly." I do a double-take. "What regenerative capabilities?"

"Are you also aware that in Mythology, the salamander is able to go through fire without any harm?"

"No, I didn't know – "

"Are you also aware that you are also able to endure mythological conflagrations without harm?"

"Are you saying that crises are – "

"Often of your own making. Often in your head."

"Maybe even an excuse to smoke a cigarette."

"Have you noticed that in the past few moments you have not smoked a cigarette, nor have you been tempted to smoke one?"

"That's true," I exclaim with surprise.

"Then you have discovered that talking to someone is a good substitute for smoking?"

"It seems to be," I say. "It's a form of procrastination I use to avoid writing."

"Then why not procrastinate to avoid smoking? Tell yourself you will have a cigarette. You will definitely have a cigarette. But not right away. Then find something else to do."

"That might work," I ponder. "But I still feel I need a cigarette with a drink or a cup of coffee. They go together. I associate them in my mind."

"Then how about switching to milk? Or tea? Something you do not associate with a cigarette?"

"You're full of very good suggestions," I observe.

"I make no suggestions," the salamander corrects me. "I simply ask questions."

"That's what Socrates said, too," I remind him.

"They accused me of corrupting the youth," the salamander recalls. "I merely wanted to show them the way to Freedom. And Truth. I channeled their abundant energy into constructive paths – dialogue, discussion, debate."

"What will I do with all the energy I release when I am no longer a smoker?" I ask.

"Ah," says the salamander, his red eyes glowing, "You have put your finger on it."

"On what?"

"On It," says the salamander. "The source. Energy."

"I don't understand," I admit.

"Then why don't you start asking questions, too?" the salamander says, and he slithers away under a rock.

CHAPTER TWENTY-FOUR
THE PEREGRINE FALCON
(Healer in the Sky)

I fell down in front of the post office, landing on my hands, knees and face. Can't sue the P.O. because it was my own stupid fault; I was wearing yukky shoes with rubber soles that caught in the rough pavement outside the building. Trying to break the fall, I sprained both wrists. Experienced headaches and pain in my nose and ears, so requested a CAT scan from the doctor.

That's when the scary part started. I didn't have a concussion, but what did show up on the scan was a small white spot on the brain. The doctor recommended an MRI. The MRI determined that I had a benign tumor, one centimeter in diameter, placed, thank heavens, where it was not interfering with mental or motor ability. The neurosurgeon did not recommend an operation, which he said might do more harm than good, but said we should watch and wait and monitor it every six months. He said if I hadn't fallen down, I might have gone my whole life without ever knowing the calcified mass was there.

Still, I did know it was there, and each night I had trouble falling asleep, seeing that X-ray in front of me with the dratted white spot where it had no business being. I decided I would try my best to take my health into my own hands and ask for divine guidance as to a medical course of action.

I had done this twice before, with good result. Since I'm a cancer survivor, I was unable to get health insurance when I moved to Florida, the idea of the insurance companies being that they will only insure those individuals who don't really need it. So I had to stay healthy, and when I needed medical expertise, I consulted the great physician in the sky.

The first time I did this, I had a wart that would not go away. It had started as an irritation on the joint of my thumb, was unsightly and red, and itched like the devil. I tried cortisone cream and every other anti-wart concoction I could get over the counter. But almost a year had gone by and the wart was still with me. I asked in meditation what I could do about it, and the reply came in two resounding words: "Spinach juice." Having resolved not to question my "medwords," I went out and bought fresh spinach, cooked it, and applied mashed leaves to my thumb. Within a few days, the wart had disappeared. Later, I told a friend of mine who dabbles in herbal and holistic medicine about it. She looked up "warts" in a book she had, and told me that the recommended specific was a plant in the spinach family.

The only other major problem I experienced was recurrent arthritis pain. I was told by my doctors, back when I had doctors, that I had osteoarthritis and it was irreversible. I did not want to get hooked on aspirin, ibuprofin, or other medications, so again I did a "help me, heaven," consult. My prescription was: "Buttermilk."

"Yuk!" was my reaction. I never drank buttermilk, and didn't think I wanted to. But next time I went shopping, I bought a quart of it and downed it with salad. The taste wasn't bad, if you didn't expect it to taste like real milk, but used it more like yogurt. I was relieved to develop a taste for it, because it chased away my arthritis pain. I don't know the medical reason for this; I don't care.

And now, I want to shrink that obnoxious tumor on my brain. I am relieved that it is benign and not malignant, since my brain is my best, if not my only, asset. But I don't like the idea of a bony intruder being there, nor the notion that it might decide to expand its territory. I go again to my meditation place, a glade in the woods, and present my symptoms to Higher Power.

* * *

Above me, I see a bird circling. It looks like a hawk. I hope it's a hawk, and not a vulture! Its wingspread is broad, and it is graceful and majestic. It makes three circles in the sky, then swoops down and lands upon my wrist. It opens its notched beak and drops a piece of paper at my feet.

"What are you?" I ask, before looking at the paper.

"I'm a peregrine falcon," it replies. "What are you?"

"From a distance, you look like a hawk," I tell the bird.

"From a distance, you look like a heap of rubbish," says the bird. I see I've got a wise-aleck on my hands.

"What does 'peregrine' mean, anyway?" I inquire.

"Pilgrim, wanderer, messenger," the falcon replies.

I pick up the message and open it. One word stares me in the face. It says "Garlic."

"Who gave you this?" I ask.

"I'm not at liberty to say," the bird answers.

"But why garlic?"

"Look," the bird snaps at me, "I don't explain the messages, I just deliver them."

"I have some garlic powder at home," I ruminate. "I wonder if that will do."

"I like things fresh, myself," the falcon says. "Bugs, baby birds, small mammals."

"You're not suggesting –?"

"Oh, no! " the falcon says. "We were merely discussing the advantages of freshness. Processing might destroy the natural ingredients. Why not go out and splurge on some garlic cloves? It's inexpensive enough." This wise old bird seems to know that one of my illnesses involves the unwillingness to spend money on myself.

"Did they tell you anything else?" I ask, fearing to go around reeking of garlic like an Italian restaurant.

"Yes, they did," the falcon responds, "but I can't quite remember it. Longish word. Silly word. I'm not as young as I used to be. It'll come to me."

"Well, I certainly hope so!" I cry. "This is important. Try to remember."

"It began with a 'C,'" the falcon says, flapping his wings as if that will stir his memory.

"Cumin, coriander, cinnamon?" I hint.

"Something like that," the falcon says.

"Oh, boy," I mutter. "You get what you pay for." I glare at the bird. "You should have told them to write it down."

"Cardamom," the bird says. "I knew I'd think of it sooner or later."

"Cardamom?" I repeat. I've cooked with many spices, but never that one.

"I think it's a form of ginger," the falcon says. "Ginger will probably do, in a pinch, but my instructions say 'cardamom'."

"Garlic and ginger," I muse. "Guess I'll be eating in Chinese restaurants for awhile."

"Suit yourself," the falcon says.

"Thank you for bringing me the message, Mr. Hawk," I say.

"Falcon," the bird corrects me.

"Oh, yes, I'm sorry." I recall that this winged messenger has had a long and colorful history, having been part of the sporting life of princes and kings for centuries.

"Some people in your country call me a 'duck hawk'," the falcon says. "And I'm related to the hawk. But I'm not a hawk, any more than you are a chimpanzee."

"I said I'm sorry," I apologize.

"Also asparagus," the bird says.

"What?"

"You heard me."

"Asparagus?"

"That's right."

"Why asparagus?"

"There you go again," the falcon says. "I think I'd better leave now, before you start asking me for recipes." The great bird spreads his striped wings, the tiger of the air, and takes off. I look again at the paper he brought me. There is nothing written on it. I take it and begin to make out a shopping list.

* * * * *

Six months later, I have another MRI. My friend Becky comes with me again, because I am scared – not only of the claustrophobic process, but of what I might hear from the doctor about the results. The doctor is all smiles. "I don't know how it happened," he says, "But your tumor has become smaller. It's down to half a centimeter."

CHAPTER TWENTY-FIVE
THE MOUSE
(Contentment)

By now, it seems, I've asked for everything there is to ask for – Love, Power, Money, Success in job – and the animals have given me their various answers. But now, as I get older, I need to know how to deal with the possibility that nothing at all might happen, that Love and Success might pass me by. So I travel in my meditation back to the woods again.

"How can I be content with what I have and no more?" I ask, and a small field mouse makes its appearance.

"I've never been rich and famous," the field mouse squeaks. "Nor have I known great love. I was interviewed once, though. By Robert Burns."

"<u>The</u> Robert Burns? The Scottish poet?"

"The same."

"Then you <u>are</u> famous. He wrote a poem about you!"

"He didn't mention my name," sighs the field mouse. He simply used the generic."

"What <u>is</u> your name? I inquire.

"Horace," says the mouse sadly.

"It probably didn't fit into his rhyme scheme," I comfort him.

"Would you like a berry?" the mouse offers . "I haven't had my breakfast."

"No, thanks," I reply "I just want to hear about you."

"No, you don't want to hear about me," the mouse says modestly. "I'm totally insignificant. Never made it into the pages of *Mouse* magazine."

"But perhaps, then, you can tell me how can I accept a life without love, without sex, without recognition."

"There are all kinds of love," says the mouse, "All kinds of sex, and all kinds of recognition. There is no such thing as a life without any form of any of them."

"I only get the rotten forms," I complain. "Why is that?"

"I cannot explain the past," says the mouse. "And I cannot tell the future. I can just tell you how to be content right now."

"Okay, how?" I ask.

"Do what I do," says the mouse.

"Eat berries?"

"You're mocking me," says the mouse, a little hurt. "But that's all right. Everybody does. I was referring to the mouse credo."

"And what is that?" I want to know. "I'm not familiar with mouse lore."

"Work," says the mouse. "And play. Fill every moment, every day."

"You've been influenced by Bobbie Burns," I observe.

"One doesn't pass through this life totally untouched by experience," says the mouse, "and I believe in sharing the benefits of one's experience."

"You are saying to concentrate on giving, not getting?"

"It's the only way," says the mouse.

"But I <u>want</u> so many things," I confess.

"That's one problem right there," says the mouse.

"Are you by any chance a Buddhist?" I query.

"I'm a gleaner," says the mouse. "I take whatever I can use, from whatever source."

"The elimination of desire...." I quote.

"Is the beginning of wisdom and contentment."

"I'll work on it," I say dubiously.

"Would you like to see me tapdance?" asks the mouse, who has finished his berries and cleaned his whiskers. The question startles me. I have never seen a tapdancing mouse before.

"All right," I agree, and make myself comfortable on a tuft of grass.

The mouse performs an excellent little routine, holding his tail draped over his left front paw. I applaud enthusiastically, and he bows, with a radiant smile.

"How did you learn to tapdance?" I ask him.

"From the snake," he explains. "It began, actually, as a hobby."

"What are you talking about?" I challenge him. "Snakes can't tap dance. Snakes don't even have feet!"

"I know," the mouse replies. "But when they chase me, I become extremely nimble. So I decided to take a class at the Senior Center."

"I see," say I. There was a pause. "Speaking of snakes," I begin.

"Do we have to?"

"I want to know –" I wonder how to put this tactfully – "Well, you mice have the reputation, which may or may not be true, of being fearful. 'Timid' is the word a mouse usually brings to mind. And Fear is one of my greatest obstacles. I mean, if I had to perform a tapdance, I would be paralyzed with Fear."

The mouse looks amazed. "Why?" he frowns.

"I'd be afraid of making a fool of myself, I suppose."

The mouse giggles. I ask him what is so funny.

"There you go again, thinking you're so important," the mouse says. "I've always known I was only one of numerous other wee creatures, so I've never had that problem. Besides, there's nothing wrong with being a fool. Just look at Mickey."

"Then, you're not really afraid of creatures who are larger and more powerful than you?"

"Not really," the mouse shrugs. "I merely avoid them." He stares at me with his head cocked to one side. "What are you afraid of right now?"

"Of dying without ever having lived," I rattle off the top of my head.

"And how is Fear going to help you?"

I stare at him dumbly. I believe it is a rhetorical question.

"Contentment," the mouse sighs, harking back to my original question. He takes a morsel of bread out of his pocket, and chews it crumb by crumb. "As the poet once said, 'A loaf of bread, a jug of wine, and thou –'"

"Oh, pooh," I snap at him. "It may be all right for a mouse to be happy with very little, but we humans always are striving for what we don't have."

"Poor you," says the mouse, shaking his little head with compassion. "I'll tell you what," he suggests. "Why don't we pretend for a moment, that you have no ego at all, that your grandiosity is gone, and that it doesn't matter what anyone else thinks of you. What would you do then?"

"Oh, that's easy," I answer. "I would do what I like to do, what I'm good at, just fill my life with happy hobbies that give me pleasure."

"And what's wrong with that?" says the mouse.

"It seems like taking the easy way out."

"Or perhaps the easy way *in*?"

"Beg pardon?

"That's my specialty - finding the easy way in – to a house, a barn, a granary, – without having to chop down any walls."

"And what does that have to do with me?"

"Why should everything worthwhile be difficult?" the mouse asks. "Puritan ethic. Calvinistic creed. Stuff and nonsense. Why not do what comes easiest to you? Other people might find what comes easily to you is difficult for them. I doubt very much that you could slide under a door jamb."

"But there's nothing I really feel passionate about right now."

"Perhaps you are in a period of rest and reevaluation," the mouse offers. "'Hibernation,' we call it. Very productive period. Adds insulation."

"I'm impatient," I complain. "I hate when nothing is happening."

"Ah," says the mouse, "But even when nothing seems to be happening, it is anyway."

I close my eyes and let the warmth of the sun bathe me in what feels like warm liquid gold. The sweet smell of pine fills my nostrils. "Mmm, that sun feels good," I say. When I open my eyes, the mouse is gone. But he has left me a note. It says, in teeny-tiny writing: "Don't forget to smell the flowers. But first you must bend down and notice them."

I look around for a snake. There is none. Even in the quiet woods, the plants keep silently growing.

CHAPTER TWENTY-SIX
THE GADFLY
(Activism)

I was heartsick over the direction my country's foreign policy was taking, and feeling helpless to do anything about it. NATO, led by the United States, was wantonly bombing Yugoslavia. Supposedly, we were concerned about Serbian treatment of Albanians. We were supposedly entering this internecine fray for "humanitarian" reasons. But since we were bombing Albanians, along with schools, hospitals, factories, monasteries, bridges, and water supplies, I suspected our actions had less to do with humanitarianism and more to do with oil and drugs. Even Alexander Haig, and he's no dove, called the Kosovo Liberation Army (which was our buddy) "drug dealers," and a respected Serbian news correspondent, the Walter Cronkite of Yugoslavia, called the K.L.A. "crack smugglers."

I stayed up late at night watching the news reports, and then I couldn't sleep. I felt we were being a bully – we were telling a small sovereign nation, "Do as we say, or we will kill you!" It bothered me that we had been unable to learn lessons from history – the Pelopponesian War, Viet Nam. Or rather, that there were two distinct historical analogies going on. One compared the Serbs to Nazis, the other compared the United States to Nazis.

What made matters worse was that I could not discuss these issues with my friends. Good "liberals" as they were, they felt they had to defend the Democrat president, no matter what foolishness he got himself and the rest of the world into. A lawyer friend of mine called the ethnic cleansing Treblinka; I call the invasion of a sovereign country, the strafing of innocent civilians Guernica. Who was right, and how can we ever make these parallel universes one?

* * *

Where can I go, but to the woods in flight, as did the Yugoslav partisans in World War II. There, in my meditation, I see wars and destruction, flames and crying babies. I hear the incessant buzzing of a missile – but it turns out not to be a missile at all. I am being visited by a gadfly.

"What can I do?" I ask the insect. "There's just one of me – I have no power, no allies – and who will listen? Every day the nation is treated to Pentagon briefings – these are the only voices we hear. What can only one person do?"

"Create a buzz," the gadfly offers gaily. "Stir up the air."

"Yes," I say. "I remember reading a book in my father's library called *The Gadfly*, by a Russian writer named Voynich. It was about a political dissident."

"Dissidents!" hisses the gadfly. "How could the universe progress, without dissidents!"

I tell him I associate this book in my mind with my father, because he was of Russian background, and he, too, was a gadfly. Like the hero of the book, who fought for Italy's freedom from Austrian rule, my father was an atheist and a rebel. A staunch moralist, he joined the Communist Party in the 1930's because he questioned the ethics of the Capitalist system; then he was thrown out of the Party in 1969, for questioning the party line about Czechoslovakia.

"A pest! A scourge! A pain in the ass! He and I would have gotten along famously!" the gadfly exults.

"Unlike him, though, I'm not part of any movement," I explain. "And I don't work for any publication; I'm a freelancer. It's frustrating, having these unpopular ideas at this time. There are so many hack journalists out there, asking the easy questions, accepting lies and evasions – and just one of me."

"There's just one of me, too," the gadfly says. "Yet I have been known to create a stampede!"

"Well," I say, "You have a weapon. A stinger."

"No, I don't," the gadfly informs me. "I'm not a bee. I don't have a stinger. I just take teeny-tiny bites. Wicked little bites that annoy the hell out of sheep and cattle."

"Mmm. So I've heard."

"You, on the other hand, do have a stinger," the gadfly says. "More than one, in fact."

"Me?"

"I believe they are called 'WORDS.'"

"Well, yes, I'm good with words," I say, "but what good does that do? I no longer have access to the media. I worked for awhile for a conservative weekly, but they kept changing my headlines to mean the exact opposite of what the story was about, so we parted company. There's only one daily newspaper in this town and they won't hire me because I'm too old, or at least, they think I am."

"I know how you feel," the gadfly commiserates. "You feel very, very small."

"Yes!" I declare. "I feel invisible and inaudible!"

"Ha," the gadfly snorts. "*You* feel small! Think of how *I* feel! Infinitesimal!"

"How do you handle that?" I ask.

"Teeny-tiny bites," the gadfly repeats.

"Anyway, who's going to listen to me?" I rant on. "I'm an unemployed teacher and unpublished writer, with absolutely no clout and no connections."

"Don't you belong to any groups whatsoever?"

"Oh, yes, I belong to a supposedly liberal church. But they regard me as a troublemaker, a pest."

"Delightful!" the gadfly grins. "I love being a pest!"

"Their Social Concerns Committee has dwindled to the chairwoman and me. If we try to start a discussion on world events, it turns into a verbal slugfest."

"Slugs," the gadfly says. "Can't stand 'em. Have no respect for them."

"No, you don't understand. I mean –" But I decide the miscommunication in the meaning of "slug" is too minor to bother correcting. "What I'm trying to tell you is that whenever I open my mouth, those people jump on me for being 'negative' and 'too critical.'"

"They're jealous of you, sweetheart," the gadfly says. "They wish they had your power."

"My what?"

"Power! There's no power like that of the pen! Mightier than the sword, and all that! And you've got it. If you choose to use it."

"But I don't really want to get into battles with people."

"Why not?" the gadfly urges. "The only way to make one's presence felt is to draw a little blood."

"I don't really mean to be a critic," I apologize.

"Why not?" goads the gadfly. "You do it so well!"

"Someone once said that a critic has no friends."

"Friends depends. There's such a thing as good criticism and bad criticism, constructive criticism and destructive criticism. I'm sure you and I can cite examples of both."

"I can," say I, "but I'd like to know what you consider 'bad' criticism."

"Those who sharpen their wits on someone else's reputation. Those who put cleverness above compassion. Those who find it easier to destroy than to create."

"The temptation is always there," I concede, "to wield the power of the pen and the advantage of an analytic mind in a swashbuckling and reckless fashion. But I try to be fair, to keep forever in front of me my motivation for the criticism."

"Which is?"

"Based on the Jewish principle of 'Tikkun Olam' – to heal the world – I try to offer suggestions that will heal."

"And have you been successful at this?" the gadfly asks. "Have your suggestions ever been used to make a situation or an organization better?"

"Often," I tell him. I give him examples: The seating arrangements at the church; the creation of genre subgroups at the Writer's Association – "But it usually takes between one and ten years for the suggestion to be implemented."

"Par for the course," the gadfly says. "We move faster than others. But they catch up eventually."

* * * * *

Inspired by my new friend, the gadfly, I wrote a letter to the editor of the local paper, suggesting that our aims in Kosovo were not what the spinmeisters claim led them to be, and that in reality the NATO war was not about Yugoslavia, it was about the military takeover of the United States. I challenged the readers to return their country to civilian control. It was hyperbole, but, as the gadfly instructed, it was meant to "draw a little blood." Many people shunned me after my letter appeared I was removed from the e-mail joke lists of five people at the church. That was okay; in the current political environment, I did not feel like reading jokes. However, a few days after my letter appeared in the paper, I received a couple of calls from local peace groups. I was added to their e-mail lists, and received daily updates from alternative news sources about what was really going on in the Balkans. We organized a teach-in.

The gadfly was right. Words are like pebbles thrown into a stream. Each one creates ripples that spread wider and wider. We never know, in fact, how far they reach, and who becomes influenced by them. After the teach-in, a high school girl who was there wrote a letter to the newspaper demanding our bombing and sanctions be halted since they were killing children.

I've started using my job as arts reviewer as a means of offering candid appraisals to the public about art, theatre and books, and of writing criticism that will lift the cultural standards in our community. Fan letters started coming in for my work. My boss (the "suit") took a survey to see which sites are visited the most on our domain, and Arts came out right near the top, ahead of even Classifieds and Sports. Miraculously enough, at Christmas time I got a bonus and my long-awaited raise.

CHAPTER TWENTY-SEVEN
THE ALLIGATOR
(Aging)

I was not dealing very well with the business of Aging. I minded when younger people spoke to me very loudly and distinctly, as if I were deaf and infirm. But more than that, I minded not having the energy I used to have, minded the feeling that my body's machinery was winding down. Who better to call on to guide me through my Aging angst, than a creature who's been around for the past 150 million years, a creature that ancient civilizations associated with knowledge, fecundity and power, and used as a symbol of death and rebirth?

* * *

As I sit in my meditation place – this time at the edge of a peaceful swamp, with cypress trees forming a Spanish moss canopy – a seven-foot-long alligator comes lumbering towards me. Instinctively, I get up and start backing away.

"Y'all don't have any call to be nervous, child," she says to me. "I ain't gonna do you no harm."

"But I've heard many tales about alligators attacking people," I say.

"Only in self defense," she assures me. "Or when they bother our young 'uns. Reason we have survived for centuries is that we look after our young folks."

"But you look like something out of Jurassic Park," I say. "And dinosaurs are scary."

"I ought to know what I do and do not like to eat," she smiles. "Most likely you have me confused with my carnivorous cousin, the crocodile." She snorts contemptuously.

"You do look very much alike," I tell her.

"We sure don't," she says. "My cousins who inhabit the Nile are much bigger – up to twenty-one feet – and they've got long, skinny snouts. I'm much prettier. They named the

University of Florida football team after me. You don't see any football team named the Crocodiles, now do you?"

"No," I have to admit. "But I don't follow football."

"I'm an American 'gator," my interlocutor continues. "My official name is Alligator Mississipiensus. But you can just call me Missy, for short."

"Isn't your diet pretty much the same as your cousin's?" I ask.

"No, ma'am," the alligator responds. "Humans are not normally on my menu. Once in awhile tourists will start feeding us and we lose our natural fear of people, in which case there might be an incident or two, but for the most part, we prefer seafood."

I sit back down, and look into her eyes, which closely resemble the eyes of humans. "I'm glad you're here," I tell her. "I wanted to know how to cope with Aging."

"You come to the right party, darling," the alligator says. "I'm older than dirt." She stretches out on a sunny strand and lowers her eyelids. "Go ahead, darling," she says. "I'm listening."

"First of all," I tell her, "it bothers me that people don't treat me with respect. They act as if I'm already dead, as if I'm as dense as a log."

"I'm often mistaken for a log myself," the alligator says. "But I like it that way. Invisibility can be a great asset, if you play your cards right."

"I don't see how – "

"If you want to observe the behavior of other creatures, it's better to do it unobserved," the alligator elucidates. "I like to submerge myself, or appear to be floating along obliviously and then snap! I've got a turtle for lunch!"

"But I find being ignored an insult."

"You need to develop thicker skin," the alligator advises. "Mine is so thick you could run a pike through it and I wouldn't even wince. Not once would I wince."

"Well, I don't want skin that's quite as thick as yours," I say.

"Don't tell me you're worried about losing your looks!" the alligator teases.

"Yes, that's part of the problem," I say. "Men don't look at me any more. They look through me."

"Oh honey," the alligator grins, "I lost my looks so long ago, I forget what my looks even looked like!"

"I suppose you'll find something positive to say about having wrinkles, too."

"Ain't you ever heard of turning your liabilities into assets? she asks. "Me, I was born with scales. Ugly? Sure! But useful. They help me glide through the water without a ripple. As I've told you, there are many situations that require you to attract the minimum of attention."

"I can't think of any," I say.

"Well, I don't know about you," the alligator says, "but I love to travel. I like to gad about without being at the mercy of predators. It's one of the pleasures of getting old."

"I never thought of alligators much as travelers," I say, "Except perhaps when they're made into luggage."

"That is not funny," the alligator says with a snort.

"I thought you said you had thick skin," I tease.

"I do," the alligator says. "When you ignore me, or call me names, it's no skin off my back. But when you really do take skin off my back – that's a different story entirely." She looks at me and literally hisses her disapproval.

"I'm sorry," I apologize. "I was being insensitive. You were saying – ?"

"In our society, old age has its benefits. We get the preferred sunning places on the banks and rest areas."

"It's just the other way 'round in our society," I lament. "The old have to make way for the young. And people are put off by wrinkles."

"Anybody that'd be put off by wrinkles don't deserve your money when you die. You let 'em know that, sweetheart. Old is never something to be afraid of, as long as you're rich."

"You are cold-blooded, aren't you!" I declare.

"I sure am," she says. "I don't let anything burn me up. Cool as a cucumber, that's me. Now if all that concerns you is your looks, I think I'll go back in the water and have me a swim."

"No, wait!" I call. "I haven't asked you the main thing yet."

The reptile turns around and comes back. "Well, spit it out, girl. I only have another fifty years to live."

"The main thing that bothers me about getting old," I confide, "is not having the energy to do everything I want to do."

"I understand," the alligator says. "That's why you got to conserve your energy, like I do. Learn to say no, when others want to waste your time. You don't have to give them a reason. Or if you need a reason, just say you don't have the time."

"Doesn't it bother you," I ask, "that you have to move so slowly?"

"Not at all," the alligator replies. "What's the rush? It would pay you to slow down, as well. It'd be better for your health, and it'd force you to prioritize."

"I don't think I know how to prioritize," I confess.

"Do you make lists?"

"Yes, I do," I reply eagerly. "I've been a listmaker since college. Sometimes I put down fifteen or twenty things I day I want to do."

"Well, you're certainly setting youself up for failure, sugar. High time you made your lists way shorter. Three things is all anybody needs to do in one day. Up to you to decide which three."

"And if I get tired?"

"Take naps."

"My mother always made me feel guilty about taking naps," I tell her. "'You're sleeping your life away!' she would say to me."

"Well, now that your mother ain't around, let me tell you what I b'lieve. I believe Sleep is the greatest invention since sawgrass! It'll restore and revive you, he'p you do whatever you need to do."

"That's another thing," I complain. "I'm not even sure what I should or could be doing with what time I have left."

"How about taking up a hobby? Learning something new always keeps a body young."

"Do you have a hobby?" I inquire.

"Oh, yes!" she says. "I sing."

"You sing?"

"Folk songs, operatic arias – I'm taking voice lessons. Would you like to hear me do 'Mating Call of the Horny Amphibian'?"

I don't think I have much of a choice, so I settle back with my arms around my knees and listen. The alligator opens her cavernous mouth, leans back her leathery neck and lets forth deep honking sounds that resemble a cow in labor.

The judgmental side of me is tempted to tell her that the sound she produces is more like a foghorn than a fugue, but then I realize it doesn't much matter what anyone thinks of her musical rendition; it is meant for other alligators. And I believe that at this point, after having mated, built a nest, birthed and raised her children, she doesn't even care what the other alligators think of her singing. She is having fun. And having fun, I decide, is going to be the focus of the rest of my life.

CHAPTER TWENTY-EIGHT
THE OTTERS
(Work as Play)

I was still blocked on the book I was writing. It was almost done, but I couldn't finish it. I visualized myself on talk shows and at book signings. I pictured myself buying a country house in New Hampshire and taking frequent trips to Europe and South America. In my dreams I really enjoyed the writer's life. I just couldn't finish the darn book.

I blamed my inactivity on the weather. *It's too warm and comfortable here in Tallahassee,* I said to myself, *and the pace is slower than up north.* I told myself I needed invigorating autumn winds and the feel of tingling snow on my face. *Maybe I should take a trip,* I conjectured. But then maybe if I did, I'd be so busy sightseeing I wouldn't have time to write at all. So I decided to take a trip north in my mind.

* * *

I am sitting on a rock by the edge of a river, under a bare willow tree, surrounded by fresh-fallen snow.

Suddenly I hear a little voice screeching, "Whheeee!" and looking around, I see two otters sliding down a snowy hill on the toboggan of their tails.

"What are you doing?" I ask.

"What does it look like we're doing?" Otter One, whom I shall call Otto Otter, parries. "We're playing!"

"Come on!" Otter Two, whom I shall call Carlotta Otter, calls. The two of them line up and play "Follow the Leader," while I trail on behind. Suddenly, they reverse positions, and I'm the leader. I get into funny poses and flap my hands like a looneybird.

"You see?" Otto laughs, "It's easy!"

"But what does this have to do with my book?" I ask.

The otters are joined by two more otters, whom I shall call Dottie Otter and Scotty Otter, and the four of them begin a game of tag, chasing each other around a tree.

"Everything!" chortles Otto. "Have you tried playing with your writing?"

"Playing," I reply curtly, "is for plays. That's why actors are called 'players' and people who write for the stage are called 'playwrights.'"

"Oh, no, no, no, no, no!" says Dottie Otter, doing a somersault in the snow, and then blowing the snow off her whiskers. "Playing is for everything!"

"Look, you folks don't seem to understand. I am writing a serious book."

"Serious!" yells Scotty, making a face.

"Serious!" echoes Dottie, holding on to his tail, while he scoots along, carrying her across a small pond of ice.

"She wants to get serious!" calls Otto, and he pantomimes giving Carlotta a kiss. She pantomimes giving him a smack across the face. Finally, getting into the spirit of their perpetual activity, I make a snowball and throw it at Otto. He makes one and throws it back, and soon we are all in a free-for-all.

"Freeze!" I hear Otto yell, and everyone poses silently like statues. Otto has taken pity on me. "Class, come to order!" he yells. The otters line up, sitting down, and he pretends to be the teacher.

"What is Play?" he asks. "Who can give me a definition?"

"Fun!" yells Dottie.

"Experimentation?" says Scotty.

"Games!" "Sport!" "Invention!" "Recreation!" they yell out of turn.

"All of the above," says Otto. "But the main thing is, you don't need to know in advance what's going to happen." The three others, while he was talking, have loosened the rock I'm sitting on. "For a short while, you are willing to lose control." I fall, plop! to the ground, into a snowbank.

"I have trouble," I confess, "with endings and beginnings."

"Try one," Carlotta suggests. "If it doesn't work, try another."

"The beginning as ending, the ending as beginning!"

"Five or six beginnings, five or six endings!"

"Have you heard the expression 'It's not written in stone'?"

"Yah, but – " I begin, but their crazy chorus cuts me off.

"Yabbit is a rabbit!"

"And a very bad habit!"

"I'll bet even Moses messed up a few tablets before he brought down the commandments from the mountain."

"If you ask me," Otto says, "You're trying too hard."

"But a lot is riding on my finishing this book," I tell him.

"A lot is riding on it!" yells Scotty, and the three other otters pile onto Otto's back, while he carries them around.

"Hey, you're killin' me!" Otto says. "Get offa me!" As they pile off, he turns to me and says, "See that? What just happened?"

"What just happened?"

"I had so much riding on my back I could hardly move."

"You're saying forget about the money. The fame. The fascinating people I'll meet. The new car."

"All of it."

"But it helps me to visualize – "

"Not while you're working."

"While you're working – "

"Forget about everything!"

"Except playing!"

Dottie takes a flying leap, jumps in the water, and floats on her back. They all follow her in, and do the same thing.

Suddenly Otto's feet hit an ice floe. He turns over and jumps on to it.

"Go with the floe!" he yells, floating downstream waving me goodbye.

"Go otterly wild!" adds Carlotta, swimming on after him, doing somersaults.

"Even into otter space!" Scotty says, jumping up in the air and then diving underwater.

"Don't think about what you otter do," advises Dottie. "Do what the otter does!"

"And soon your audiences will cry Otter, Otter!" they all applaud, disappearing over a cascade.

* * *

In the spirit of "Fun, Experimentation, Games, Sport, Invention and Recreation," I wrote four alternative openings for my sci fi novel and presented them to my fiction group. They liked them all, but chose one and suggested I incorporate ideas from the other segments into that one. I finished the book joyously, and it didn't finish me!

CHAPTER TWENTY-NINE
THE FLORIDA PANTHER
(Responsibility)

And then suddenly things start happening for me. My writing was starting to sell – poems and stories were accepted and a book contract was in the works. Men start coming out of the woodwork and my social life picked up. In fact, I had so many invitations, I was confused about where to go, and who with. People in town seemed to know me wherever I went, and they greeted me with respect and smiles, and something like awe. And how did I react? I was a nervous wreck. *What's going on here?* I asked myself. *I've been praying for Success, and then when I start getting some, I'm as miserable as before!*

* * *

So I wander into the woods again in my mind, and who should appear, in her glorious grace, but a tawny Florida panther.

"I had hoped for a lion," I complain. "As in Very Important Person, as in being lionized, as in King of the Jungle. You know, the kind with a mane and all."

"This isn't Africa," the lion reminds me. "This is North Florida. There aren't even any mountain lions, as in the North. I'm as close to a lion as you can get around here, and you ought to take advantage of my wisdom while you can get it, because I'm on the Endangered Species list."

"All right," I agree. "I want to know why being respected and admired and sought after is freaking me out."

"You're not used to it, I suppose," the panther says. She has a husky, throaty voice reminiscent of Lauren Bacall.

"No, I'm not," I admit. "I don't know how to handle it. It reminds me of high school, when I was used to being a wallflower, but if two boys asked me to dance, it was such a heady experience I felt drunk and wanted to run out of the place and hide."

"I hope you were polite," the lioness says.

"I don't know if I was or not? But why should I be?"

"*Noblesse oblige*," the panther sighs.

"No blessings what?" I repeat, dumbfounded.

"It's a French term," the panther explains. "It means the responsibility of those in power."

"Power?" I retreat from this very scary and threatening word.

"Isn't that what we're talking about?" the panther queries. "Originally the term referred to the obligations of the high-born, the wealthy class. But in a democracy all sorts of people can obtain power. And they, too, have obligations."

"Such as?"

"The obligation to be generous, to be honorable."

"Do you consider yourself generous and honorable?" I challenge the cat.

"I share the kill," the panther says.

"Oh, sure," I say. "After taking the lion's share."

"You seem to resent authority," the panther notes. "It's no wonder you are having trouble becoming one."

"It frightens me to have power," I confess.

"I can see that," the cat observes. "Do you perhaps feel, having been raised in a time when male chauvinist pigs were prevalent, that women should not be powerful, that they should be subservient to men and let them claim the power?"

"Well, yes, maybe I do think that," I frown. "Although I never verbalized it."

"In the cat culture," the panther informs me, "The female makes the kill."

"But doesn't that make you – well, masculine?"

The cat smiles a Mona Lisa smile. "Not in the least," she says. "It simply makes me powerful."

"And how do you handle it?" I want to know. "How do you act when everyone's treating you like a star, like a queen, like a celebrity?"

"With grace and dignity," the panther replies. She paces back and forth, allowing me to admire her lithe and streamlined movements.

"I guess I'm afraid if people look too hard, they'll find out I'm a fraud, that I'm really weak and childish inside."

"But you have your achievements to tell them otherwise," the panther says.

"And I'm afraid I won't be able to keep up the achievements and then they'll laugh at me."

"No one ever laughs at the truly strong," the panther says.

"Am I truly strong?" I ask. "Or am I just lucky?"

"Only you can answer that," the lioness replies. "But I don't believe in luck. Luck may put a deer in my path, but it is I who make the decision what to do about it."

"Nonsense!" I cry. "What if I won the lottery? That would be luck, wouldn't it?"

"First, you would have to purchase a ticket," the panther says.

"Well, yes, but then – "

"And then you would have to decide how to spend the money."

"Oh, I know how I would spend the money!" I cry.

"Do you?" the cat smirks. "Or would you fritter it all away, feeling unworthy of winning it to begin with?"

"I don't know – I – "

"Recognition and success is just like winning the lottery. Now it's time to remember all the wonderful things you wanted to do if and when you became successful."

"You're making it sound like work," I say.

"It is," says the panther. "You just have a bigger job than you had before."

"A job? Being successful is a job?"

"Of course it is," the lioness says. "Has no one come to you for help?"

"Well, yes, they have," I recollect. "They ask me for advice. They want me to protect them. They want me to introduce them to people."

"Sounds like work," the lioness says, throwing my comment back at me.

"I am not used to being in this position," I say.

"Then get used to it," the lioness says. "But remember, you are still the same person you were before."

"That's the trouble. I'm afraid all my faults will be magnified."

"So they will," says the lioness. "But so will your good points. You will be able to be more of what you always wanted to be."

Something occurs to me, a memory from childhood, that I want to share with my new friend. "Can I tell you a secret?" I ask.

"Go ahead," the panther says. "I've just had lunch. I'm in no hurry to go anywhere."

"My parents were very scary, very domineering," I confide. "If I ever went against them, I got stepped on. Fast. They were the power figures in the family. My survival depended on my placating them, and on not attracting too much attention."

"Attention, is it?"

"Yes," I go on. "I dressed in a manner to be inconspicuous, I spoke in a whisper, I never bragged about myself or my accomplishments. I did not want to bring down their wrath upon me."

"Now let me tell you a secret," the panther says. "There is a certain respect, a certain *je ne sais quoi*, that comes with an office. When you are the president of an organization, people treat you as the president. When you are a published writer, people treat you as a published writer. When you are beautiful and famous, people will admire you and want to emulate you."

"And what do I do about that?" I ask.

"Nothing," the panther smiles serenely. "Nothing at all. Enjoy it, and accept it."

"But people will expect me to know everything, to do everything."

"That's their problem, not yours," the cat shrugs.

"But who can I go to for counsel?" I ask. "Haven't you heard the expression 'It's lonely at the top'?"

"You move up to a different set of advisors," the lioness instructs. "You tap the experts. And don't forget, you can still go to the very top and ask God."

"Yes," I say, hanging my head in embarrassment, "I forgot about that."

"The tendency is," the lioness says, "to believe, once you are in power, that you *are* God. In order to maintain your balance and your perspective, I suggest you continue your constant contact with powers higher than yourself."

"Thank you," I say. 'I will!"

"One more thing," the panther says.

"Yes?"

"Have you observed how softly I tread?"

"Well, no, I – "

"Too busy thinking about yourself, I suppose," the lioness says. "Well, please benefit from my experience. In order not to incur the wrath of the jealous – and that is really the only thing a lion has to worry about – fighting with hyenas – one must be a little mysterious. Don't flaunt your wealth or your abilities."

"*Noblesse oblige*," I reiterate.

"Exactly," purrs the cat. She leaps onto a rock and poses for a moment – a magnificent sight – before disappearing into the wilds.

CHAPTER THIRTY
THE BUTTERFLY
(Dealing with Mortality)

Something was happening in my relationships that I didn't like. I found myself not wanting to hear about the successes of my friends. I didn't want to know that Ludy was in a play, and that June was working on a marvelous piece of investigative journalism. I was not aware of the depth of my feeling until I attended a St. Patty's Day concert and saw someone I knew from the writers' association playing three different instruments – fiddle, guitar and hand-held drum. I first met her when it was my task to give her a prize for writing a winning story in our fiction contest, and I happened to know she was also enrolled for an advanced degree in the English program at the University. She was also an expert quilter. When she went to the microphone and started singing a plaintive Irish melody in a voice like an angel, my eyes welled up with tears. Tears of what? Envy? Despair at my own lack of achievement? Longing for my lost energy? Regret for the fact that I am getting old, and the future is looking more and more like an empty room?

One night I dreamed about Death. I was on board a ship and we were pulling into a port called *Havre de Grace*, or Harbor of Grace. I could hear people singing *Anima e Cuore,* an Italian song that means "Body and Soul." But there were no people anywhere around. When I woke up, my heart was pounding with fear.

* * *

I don't even want to go in my meditation to the woods. I want to stretch out in a meadow, letting the sun warm me like a mother nursing her baby. I breathe deeply, inhaling the scent of clover. In the distance, I hear the sound of birds; up close, I hear buzzing insects. I refuse to open my eyes. I am playing dead. At last, a tiny, feathery, musical voice asks me, "Well? How long are you going to lie there?" I open my eyes, and on the calyx of a sunflower, see a gigantic butterfly.

"What's the use of getting up, going anywhere, doing anything?" I sigh. "Nothing good will come of it. I'll only be rejected – again – only be made to feel that the world is passing me by."

"I'm sorry," the butterfly says. "But I don't understand your problem."

"My problem is," I snap with great annoyance, "that I don't have much time left."

"None of us do," the butterfly sighs. "But what do you need time for?"

"To fulfill all the dreams I had when I was young. To make some sort of contribution, before I, before I – "

"I see," the butterfly says with hesitation. I doubt she had sustained many long-range goals when she was a caterpillar. I feel I might even be wasting time right now, even talking with her.

"How much time do you have, exactly?" she asks.

"I don't know," I cry in anguish. "But whatever it is, it won't be enough!"

"I have had less than one year," the butterfly says. "And today is my last day."

I stare at her, and feel remorse at my insensitivity. But she is actually smiling. "How do you handle that?" I ask, "Knowing that the end is near?"

"I do the only thing that I can do," she says.

"And what is that?"

"I seek beauty, I create beauty, I am beauty."

"How do you define 'beauty'?" I ask.

"I don't," the butterfly says, waving her shimmering wings. "I let others do that."

'You are indeed quite lovely," I acknowledge begrudgingly, aware that my own looks are beginning to fade.

"Exquisite," the butterfly corrects me.

"What?"

"I've been told that I am exquisite," she says demurely.

"Yes, maybe," I grumble. "I don't give lavish compliments."

"Would you like to spend the day with me?" the butterfly asks. I tell her I am flattered she has chosen me to share her last precious moments.

I don't know whether I shrunk in size like Alice in Wonderland, or the flying stained glass window grew, but I find myself astride her back, circling over a beautiful garden.

"Where are we going?" I ask.

"I don't know," she replies cheerily.

"You mean, we are just going to drift, from here on out?"

"I like to call it 'purposeful drifting,'" she says.

"But – " I begin, my Puritan work ethic kicking in.

"But me no buts," she says. "Today let us know only 'ands'." Suddenly, she becomes animated. "Look down there!" she cries. "Red, red, red!"

"A rose garden," I observe.

"Oh, let's go visit the Roses!" she suggests. We drop in on a family of vibrant red roses, and they serve us a lovely nectar for tea. We have a lively discussion about great women named Rose, starting with my Grandma Rosie and Rosie the Riveter, up to and including Rosa Bonheur, the painter, and Rosa Luxemburg, the fighter for Labor and Women's Rights.

We then call on the Lantanas, who are having a crocheting contest. They encourage everyone to participate, and though I've never crocheted before, I manage to make a hat for myself, in the saffron and orange colors of the Lantana.

"See if it fits!" my butterfly companion urges. And it does. Perfectly.

"Aren't you going to make something?" I ask.

"I used to be a weaver," she informs me. "But that's a task for a young chrysalis. I'm happy to admire their handiwork."

"Are you really?" I challenge her. "Don't you find yourself just the slightest bit jealous?"

"Oh, heavens no!" she says. "For the older I get, the more skills and wisdom I acquire! I can measure the heat and light of the sun! I can ride the surf of ocean waves! And, of course, I am a social butterfly."

The lacy petals of The Lantanas are becoming quite crowded, for they are a veritable salon for butterflies. A very handsome gentleman butterfly, a Monarch, elegantly attired, approaches my lady friend. They bow to each other a few times, and he folds and unfolds his magnificent wings to impress her, then sprays her with a sweet-smelling perfume. She laughs coquettishly. My friend comes over and tells me they're going for a spin and she'll be back in awhile. I watch them fly off together, and turn my attention back to the other lepidoptera, who are now having flying races for the men, while the females trade pollen recipes.

In mid-afternoon, my butterfly comes back and tells me it is time for her to search for a sturdy milkweed plant on which to lay her eggs. While she does so, I hear a small bird chirping, close to me on the ground. I see a baby oriole who has fallen from its nest and bruised its wing. Remembering what the wolf told me, about being of assistance even to those of other species, I take the wee thing in the cup of my hand, clamber up the nearby tree and replace the bird in its nest. Its mother circles around in agitation, then comes up to me and rests her head next to my hand in gratitude.

"That was a beautiful thing you did," one of the butterflies says to me. "Perhaps even more beautiful than the hat."

"I just did what I had to do," I say, embarrassed.

"Yes," she says, "That is what heroes do. There is beauty in generous deeds."

As twilight begins to fall, my butterfly returns. She seems weary. She has torn her wing on a thistle. But the music of the crickets, who are striking up their percussion orchestra, enchants her.

"Ah, a concert!" she exclaims. We sit and listen as the sky darkens, and watch the fireflies illuminate the sky like little stars. I glance over to the butterfly to see if she's getting nervous as her allotted doom approaches, but she is rapt in the music.

"Aren't you afraid of Death?" I whisper to her.

"What's Death?" she asks.

"Being no more," I explain to the innocent, astonished she's never heard of The Grim Reaper.

"We don't call it 'Death,'" she says. "We call it 'Making Room.'"

"Making Room?" I repeat, befuddled.

"Just imagine how terrible it would be if Earth were cluttered with millions of sick old butterflies and there were no room for the children to play!"

"But having to leave one's home, one's friends," I mourn, "Having to give up all of one's hopes and expectations –"

"I have had my life," she says matter-of-factly. "I have known love and friendship. I have performed service to the flowers who fed me. I have gone through many changes; I have learned to dance. I have traveled with the wind – down to Mexico and back. And I will leave young ones to come after me. It is not the length of one's life that's important," she reminds me, "it's the quality of life." That long speech seems to have caused her to have a coughing spell. She flutters her wings helplessly, and I sense that her time has come.

"You are not only Beauty," I whisper to her, "you are Joy."

"And so are you, my dear child of God," she smiles, folding her elegant wings once more, and falling, falling to the ground.

EPILOGUE

I am not magic, I am not chosen by angels, I am not a religious fanatic, I am not insane, and I am not a liar. I am not special in any way in my ability to channel conversations with spiritual guides. You can do it, too. Anybody can. All it takes is an openness and a belief that the universe holds answers for you that it is all too willing to share. It requires nothing more than acceptance of your own powers and the powers of nature. Miracles can happen if you expect them, and if you adopt the motto: "Accept first, question later."

There is nothing to fear, because meditations (and that's what these are) are like dreams, and as a wonderful dream analyst once told me, "There is no such thing as a bad dream." Even dreams which might seem like nightmares are given to your psyche to teach you a lesson or to point the way to new and constructive action.

So, find a time and a place to meditate, with a view to plugging in to the great spiritual web, and see what the universe has to say to you.

Printed in the United Kingdom
by Lightning Source UK Ltd.
9480600001B